Praise for SPANISH FOR CRUISERS
...from cruisers with over 200 years of cruising experience

"SPANISH FOR CRUISERS is like our right hand when we are in Spanish-speaking countries. Kathy's style of teaching gets you speaking out on the street. If you ever see a class being given, don't miss it."
— Diane and Harold Clapp, s/v *Sea Camp*

"Anyone who is going to the Dominican Republic or any Spanish-speaking country should carry SPANISH FOR CRUISERS with them."
— Stephen Pavlidis, author of THE EXUMA GUIDE, THE ABACO GUIDE, THE CENTRAL AND SOUTHERN BAHAMAS GUIDE, THE TURKS AND CAICOS GUIDE

"SPANISH FOR CRUISERS, wow! Kathy Parsons uses the K.I.S.S. principal, "keep it simple system," as I profess in m cookbooks. Chuck says this book will be a major help to us in our travels. Especially important is the book layou format. Easy to read, easy to comprehend, just the right words about parts, measurements, ordering and all the that we cruisers want and need and are not easily found or understood in the conventional source materials. A pronunciation guide is among the 25 specific categories that are specifically geared for us, the cruisers. With thi we will have a much easier time dealing with mechanics, vendors, officials and the public in Spanish-speaking l We have a bunch of Spanish/English dictionaries including an electronic gadget, but none even come close to tl user-friendliness of SPANISH FOR CRUISERS by Kathy Parsons."
— Corinne C. Kanter author, *The Galley K.I.S.S. Cookbook and The (K.I.S.S. Cookbook*, Charles E. Kanter, AMS, author lecturer, Marin Surveyor, ex-delivery skipper and chronic cruiser.

"A unique concept put forth in a highly usable format. A must for every bookshelf of Caribbean cruisers. Thou geared primarily to mechanical situations, Kathy's book gives a good basic background in conversational Spani everyday use."
— Monty and Sara Lewis, authors, EXPLORER CHARTBOOKS

M0001121758

...continued

"I've spoken Spanish for fifty years ... I just bought SPANISH FOR CRUISERS and learned more from it about boats and their nomenclature in Spanish than 50 years of experience."

— Captain Magic, s/v *Inca*

"First law of cruising: Something always breaks. Second law of cruising: It usually breaks at an inconvenient time in an unfamiliar place. That's why SPANISH FOR CRUISERS is an absolutely essential book for the shipboard library. It's organized so you can find the phrases you need - FAST!... SPANISH FOR CRUISERS is as easy to use as uno, dos, tres — even if those are the only Spanish words you know... It will pay for itself dozens of times over."

— Ann Vanderhoof and Steve Manley
Publishers, The PORTS Cruising Guides

"SPANISH FOR CRUISERS is the greatest for boaters heading for Spanish-speaking countries. There is nothing else out there that will tell you how to order a new impeller or alternator brushes or ... It's terrific!"

— Mary and Christian Verlaque, s/v *I Wanda*

"Parsons' book fills a real need for cruisers. This unique and easy-to-use tool will save you hours of frustration and possibly buckets of money."

— Eileen Quinn, cruiser s/v *Little Gidding* and recording artist,
NO SIGNIFICANT FEATURES, DEGREES OF DEVIATION

"For going down-island, this is one of the most practical books we have on our boat. Not only practical but well laid-out and easy-to-use. Very complete."

— Bill and Donna Lott, s/v *Sweet Success*

"SPANISH FOR CRUISERS is terrific - the ultimate definition of cruising "repairing your boat in exotic places" now can take place in exotic Spanish-speaking places."

— Jim and Edwina Young, s/v *Jasper J*

Spanish for Cruisers:

BOAT REPAIRS AND MAINTENANCE PHRASE BOOK

Buen viaje
Kathy

Practical Spanish vocabulary and expressions for
⚓ handling boat emergencies and repairs
⚓ finding hardware and parts
⚓ communicating with boatyards, mechanics, sailmakers, repairmen

⚓

Kathy Parsons

AVENTURAS Publishing Company
Hallettsville, Texas

Spanish for Cruisers: Boat Repairs and Maintenance Phrase Book

Practical Spanish vocabulary and expressions for handling boat emergencies and repairs, finding hardware and parts, and communicating with boatyards, mechanics, sailmakers, and repairmen.

by Kathy Parsons

Published by: **Aventuras Publishing Company**
AVENTURAS   Rt. 4 Box 180
Hallettsville, Texas 77964
email: kathy@spanish4cruisers.com
(361) 798-4159

All rights reserved. This book may not be duplicated in any way without the expressed written consent of the publisher, except in the form of brief excerpts or quotations for the purposes of review. The information contained herein is for the personal use of the reader, and may not be incorporated in any commercial programs, other books, information storage and retrieval systems, or any kind of software without written consent of the publisher or author. Making copies of this book, for any purpose other than your own, is a violation of United States copyright laws.

Copyright © 2000 by Kathy Parsons.

Cover design and artwork: **Mari's Graphical Environments**
Mari M. Hiltz   140 Tomahawk Drive #67
Indian Harbour Beach, FL 32937
email: dmhiltz@iu.net   web: www.foreversoon.com
Phone: (407) 773-0920

Illustrations: Dorothy Bujnoch
Cartoon: Chuck Butler

● ●

Library of Congress Cataloging-in-Publication Data

Parsons, Kathy
    Spanish for Cruisers: Boat Repairs and Maintenance Phrase Book :
Practical Spanish vocabulary and expressions for handling boat
emergencies and repairs, finding hardware and parts, and communicating
with boatyards, mechanics, sailmakers, and repairmen. / Kathy Parsons -
1st ed.
        p.   cm.
        Includes index and illustrations.
   ISBN 0-9675905-0-7
   1. Spanish language—Conversation and Phrase Books
   I. Title
PC4121.P37 2000
468.3'421—dc20   99-067832
                                              CIP

Please don't copy this book. If your friends want a copy, please e-mail, phone, or write to Aventuras Publishing at the address shown above. We can give you information on ordering or direct you to stores where Spanish for Cruisers is carried.

Printed in the United States of America

Limits of Liability and Disclaimer of Warranty
The author and publisher of this book have used their best efforts in preparing this book. The author and publisher make no warranty of any kind, expressed or implied, with regard to the information contained in this book. The author and publisher shall not be liable in any event of incidental or consequential damages in connection with, or arising out of, the use of the material.

For Dave

Table of Contents

Table of Contents

Table of Contents

Out of the Mouths of Cruisers..... *(True Stories!)*

Hey, Toilet! Throw me your clothes!

Excusado! Tire su ropa!

Cruiser to the author of this book:	**You know, I've been saying "Excusado!" for "Excuse me" but I seem to get funny looks.**	
She meant:	**Excuse me!**	
She really said:	**Toilet !**	*(excusado is a euphemism for **toilet**; use Perdón or Disculpe for **Excuse me**)*
Cruiser to the official on the dock in Cuba:	**Tire la ropa!**	
She meant:	**Throw me the rope!**	
She really said:	**Throw me your clothes!**	*(**ro**pa = clothes; use **ca**bo or **so**ga for **rope**)*
Author to the hairdresser cutting her mate's hair:	**Córtele el culo!**	
She meant:	**Cut off his ponytail!**	
She really said:	**Cut off his ass!**	*(**co**la = ponytail, **cu**lo = ass, Freudian slip...?)*

Table of Contents

Acknowledgments

Gracias!

Sometimes it seems there isn't a person on this planet who hasn't helped me with this book. I carried this book in my backpack and solicited help from almost everyone. I pulled this book out throughout the Caribbean and asked fellow cruisers to practice pronouncing the phonetics. Many boaters, at various levels of Spanish, spent hours reviewing the material in this book page-by-page, telling me what I was missing, and what needed to be made clearer. Spanish-speaking mechanics, sailmakers, shopkeepers, engineers, dockmasters, officials, and just plain nice people reviewed the vocabulary and helped me find the best, simplest way to get a point across.

Mil gracias *(a thousand thanks)* **to all the Spanish speakers and Latin American businesses that reviewed and helped with the editing of this book, including:**

Charlie Adam, Venezuela Marine Supply (Vemasca), Margarita, Venezuela
Bahía Redonda Marina, Puerto La Cruz, Venezuela
Emilia Barboza, Venezuela
Juan Baró, ship's agent, Margarita, Venezuela
Leilane Escobar, college student, Mexico
Fanny, cruiser from Venezuela
Fidel Folchi, engineer, Venezuela
Carlos González, Astur Baja Services, San José del Cabo, Baja California, Mexico, and San Antonio, Texas
Giorgi Neri, boatyard owner, Navimca, Cumaná, Venezuela
Rosario, marine diesel mechanic from the Dominican Republic
Sailing Shop, Margarita, Venezuela
Rafael Sierra, mechanic, Cummins Southeastern Power, Hialeah, Florida; First Machinist, Cuba
Simón, canvaswork and sail repair, Margarita, Venezuela
Ventura, s/v Blue Bottle, cruiser from Spain
Chris Wooley, The Shop – El Toque Final, Río Dulce, Guatemala

●●●

Many cruisers (too many to list here) have reviewed SPANISH FOR CRUISERS, *taken my classes, tested the course materials and offered countless suggestions. I would like to offer special thanks to the following:*

Chuck and Barb Butler, s/v *Tiara Lee*, Diane and Harold Clapp, *s/v Sea Camp;* Mike and Pat Davidson, s/v *Impulse;* Ken De Pree, *s/v Halcyon;* Rob Dubin, *s/v Ventana;* Mari Hiltz, s/v *Forever Soon;* Bernie and Yvonne Katchor, s/v *Australia 31;* Sarah Lewis, m/y *Saranade;* Bruce and Roxie MacKinnon, s/v *Boundless,* Betsy Morris, s/v *Salsa;* Nancy Newton, s/v *La Esmeralda*

Special thanks for editing goes to Peggy Livingston.

And to all my students whose enthusiasm motivated me to create this book. My students were excellent about field-testing our class material each day on the streets and reporting back where they succeeded and what problems they encountered. In addition, they helped me figure out the best way to cover aspects of Spanish that typically confuse English-speakers.

To Dave who encouraged this book, helped in many ways, and traveled through many of these countries with me. And to George and Dorothy Bujnoch.

You too can help!

Be one of SPANISH FOR CRUISERS' field researchers. Write and let me know how you have used this book. Do you have suggestions, corrections, additional words and phrases that you think should be added to future editions? Let me know where different Spanish words are used locally in countries that you visit. Send a funny or enlightening story on your experiences speaking Spanish. Or ask questions about the material in SPANISH FOR CRUISERS.

Email Kathy Parsons at kathy@spanish4cruisers.com. Or write to: Kathy Parsons, Route 4 Box 180, Hallettsville, TX 77964. Or just dinghy over to s/v *Romance* if you see her at anchor!

Acknowledgments

My favorite Spanish classes are the ones where I take a few students to the streets on a **mission**. We may go to the hardware store, the produce market, or a restaurant. Before we head out, I'll work out a strategy with my students: *"These are the best ways to ask this question... When the clerk tells you the price, parrot it back to him immediately in Spanish so he can confirm that you heard the numbers correctly..."* As we enter the store, I prompt them with the vocabulary they will need to talk to the clerk or the waiter. If they need another word, I whisper it to them.

Since I can't cruise with you, I've tried to do the same thing in this book. I've tried to give you a companion that you can carry in your backpack, that will give you the phrases and vocabulary you need for your various "missions" to the hardware store, the boatyard, or the outboard mechanic.

I had to make this book easy to use so that it would be almost as accessible as your own personal Spanish teacher. Vocabulary is organized by topic in English with translation and pronunciation of each Spanish word or phrase. There is a Quick Reference guide on the cover flap and a detailed Table of Contents to help you navigate the book. In addition, every English word is included in the index at the end of SPANISH FOR CRUISERS, so you can always find what you need quickly.

Many pages include diagrams of the hardware covered on that page. These will help you find the right page and may even help you communicate in a crunch. I'm not proud – I won't be offended if someday you choose to just point to a picture in the book, and say *"Hay?" (Is there?")* or *"¿Cuánto cuesta?" (How much does it cost?")*. The important thing is that you get out there and communicate. Every time you get out there and successfully use a little Spanish, your success will build on itself and the words will flow easier the next time.

● ●

Definition of *Cruising*: "Doing BOAT MAINTENANCE in Exotic Places"

I originally planned to include this mechanics and hardware-related vocabulary as a small section in the SPANISH FOR CRUISERS: GENERAL CONVERSATION PHRASE BOOK I was writing. However, as I began to list the words and phrases you need to know to handle boat breakdowns and emergencies and to communicate with mechanics, boatyards, sailmakers, and hardware store clerks, I realized just how much there was to cover. As I showed this growing list to fellow cruisers, they all responded "Boy, I'd love to have that list – all of it."

If you've been out cruising awhile, you know that eventually things on your boat break or require maintenance. Our engine's fresh water pump seized just North of Honduras. We had to find a mechanic to help us press the bearings out and a welder to repair a crack in the housing. We hauled the boat in Guatemala and painted the bottom and fixed the rudder. We purchased refrigerant for our refrigeration system economically in Guatemala City. A number of cruisers took advantage of the excellent hardwoods and carpenters in Guatemala and had their hatches and companionway boards replaced. In Margarita, Venezuela, we had the genoa restitched at a very reasonable price. Other boaters commissioned dinghy covers, awnings, cushions and new sacrificial strips for their roller furling jib. Obviously, I could go on and on relating all the projects that fellow cruisers chose to do or were forced to do while cruising in Spanish-speaking countries – from engine rebuilds to re-teaking the decks.

Ideally, you want to feel comfortable maintaining and repairing your boat with the help of the local economy. You want to be able to take advantage of the inexpensive, skilled labor and often excellent local materials available in these countries. You want to handle projects smoothly to give you more time to enjoy the countries you came to visit.

SPANISH FOR CRUISERS provides this essential boating, hardware and mechanical vocabulary that is hard to find elsewhere. You won't find it in your Spanish-English dictionary. Where you do find some of the terms, they tend to list words that are used in Spain and are often unknown in the Americas. The vocabulary in this book has been extensively tested by cruisers and reviewed by Spanish speaking mechanics, boatyard owners, canvasworkers, and shopkeepers in the countries you will be visiting.

Overview How to Jump-Start Your Spanish

This book is primarily a phrase and vocabulary book. I'm not trying to teach you Spanish grammar and sentence structure. (For that, you will need the companion LESSON BOOK in the SPANISH FOR CRUISERS series.) However, to get the most out of this book, spend a little time with the Chapters 1, 2, 3, and 4. These are:

Chapter 1: Using the Vocabulary Pages

The vocabulary pages follow a consistent format throughout this book to make SPANISH FOR CRUISERS as quick and easy to use as possible. Review Chapter 1 to learn how to use these pages and the pronunciation guides to the best advantage.

Chapter 2: Pronunciation

I consider pronunciation to be so important that I deal with it twice. First, every Spanish word and phrase in this book has its Spanish pronunciation listed in the right-hand column on every page. But, in addition, I have provided you with an overview of the rules of Spanish pronunciation in Chapter 2. Take the time to read this chapter. Practice pronouncing the Spanish words with a Spanish speaker who can correct your pronunciation. It will help your Spanish immensely. Your pronunciation will improve and you will tend to learn new words faster because you will quickly associate their pronunciation with their spelling.

Chapter 3: Basic Conversation

This chapter contains the Spanish phrases that you will use on a daily basis. They are essential in any Spanish conversation. These will allow you to create sentences on your own and build your conversational skills. Learn and practice as many of these as you can. Some of these phrases are listed again inside the back cover as a quick reference.

© 2000 Kathy Parsons, Spanish for Cruisers

Learn the basic greetings and phrases of courtesy such as "*please, thank you, excuse me*, and *you're welcome*" and use them every chance you get. Greet people you pass on the streets and certainly those you approach in a store. Say please and thank you. Not only will your Spanish hosts call you courteous, but you will find that these simple Spanish phrases loosen your tongue and make it easier for you to get out those more difficult Spanish words. When it comes to learning a foreign language, silence is *not* golden. You want these basic greetings and courtesies to become old hat, so that you can concentrate on the substance of your conversation. Spanish proficiency comes to those with the courage to get out there and try their Spanish. Spanish speakers *always* appreciate your efforts.

Chapter 4: Numbers and Money

Want to annoy your crew members while performing a noble activity? Practice counting aloud in Spanish. It's great for your pronunciation and helps you learn your numbers. Much of our Spanish ashore involves numbers – most particularly prices. Use the tricks presented in this book to become confident that you understand the number or price you were given. This will eliminate a very common cruising frustration *"But I thought he told me yesterday that it would cost ...?"* Are you being taken advantage of, or did you just misunderstand? Of course, you can also ask them to "write it down, please" *(Es·crí·ba·lo, **por** fa·**vor**).*

The Rest of the Book...

You will find Chapters 5 through 8 useful for almost any kind of Spanish conversation ashore. Chapter 5 gives you the basic conversational skills you need for shopping. Chapter 6 presents a useful strategy and the vocabulary you need to find your way around. Chapter 7 teaches you to set times for appointments. If you ever find yourself in need of emergency help at sea, Chapter 8 will give you the phrases you need to call for help, identify yourself and location, and specify the assistance you require. From Chapter 9 on, you will find the terms you need for different types of repair and maintenance. Consult these chapters as you need them.

© 2000 Kathy Parsons, Spanish for Cruisers

1   Keep this book by the nav station. If you ever need to get help while you are at sea, use the **EMERGENCIES** section to communicate over the VHF, SSB, or with a boat that you flag down.

*Read the **EMERGENCIES** section now. Highlight the sentences that refer to your boat and crew. Fill in the information on your boat's length, draft, and beam, so you will be ready to talk if you ever need to get help quickly.*

2   Carry this book in your backpack whenever you go to the hardware store, boatyard, or mechanic. Open this book to the appropriate page and use the phonetics to pronounce the words and phrases you need. If you're having a bad-mouth day and just can't get the tongue to move, point to the phrases you'd like to say or point to the picture of the item you are looking for.

*By the way, Spanish-speakers **love** this book. They too have been frustrated by their inability to communicate with "gringos" (English-speakers), and are usually quite interested in learning some English words. Also, they find our attempts at writing out Spanish phonetics hilarious.*

3   If you are new to Spanish, the most useful thing you can do is to master the rules of Spanish pronunciation. Read and practice pronouncing all the Spanish words on the pronunciation pages in Chapter 2. The more practice you can get speaking Spanish aloud, the easier it gets, and the better you sound!

© 2000 Kathy Parsons, Spanish for Cruisers

*Find a Spanish-speaking person to sit down with you and listen to you pronounce the words in this book. Your friend doesn't even have to know English. He or she only needs to be able to read and speak Spanish. Single-handers, this is an **excellent** way to break the ice with interesting strangers!*

4. Review the book and highlight the words and phrases that you will use most. Practice pronouncing them aloud. Since this book is organized in columns, it is easy, for example, to cover columns 2 and 3 to see if you remember the Spanish word and pronunciation for the English word in the first column. Pay special attention to Chapter 3 – Basic Conversation and learn and use as many of these phrases as you can.

Your Spanish-speaking friend can help you with this too!

5. Buy an extra copy of this book and give it to the Spanish-speaking mechanic, boatyard owner, or repairman who has gone out of his way to be helpful to you. This book will help them work with English-speaking boaters more effectively.

I received enthusiastic help from every Spanish-speaking boatyard owner, dockmaster, canvas worker and mechanic that I approached. Everyone has wanted to help me complete this book so that they can get a copy of it. There is nothing like this for Spanish-speakers who want to learn to do work for English-speaking cruisers.

© 2000 Kathy Parsons, Spanish for Cruisers

Vocabulary words and phrases are organized in three columns in this book:

① *English*	② *Spanish*	③ *Spanish pronunciation*
Where is the ...?	¿Dón·de es·tá el ... ?	Dohn-deh ehss-tah ehl ...?
Is there a ... nearby?	¿Hay un ... cer·ca?	Eye oon ... sehr-kah?

① *English word or phrase*

Whenever you see "...", you may substitute a word or phrase of your choice. For example,
Is there a ... nearby?
Is there a *hardware store* nearby?
Is there a *bank* nearby?

In some instances, the word is substituted in different places in the English and Spanish versions of a phrase. Use the locations of the "..." as your guide to inserting the phrase in the correct place in the sentence.

② *Spanish translation*

Each Spanish word is divided into syllables with a small dot. Pronounce each word slowly, syllable by syllable. There is no harm whatsoever in speaking slowly. You may have a tendency to leave out a syllable or two when pronouncing long Spanish words. This will help you avoid that tendency.

© 2000 Kathy Parsons, Spanish for Cruisers

In any word, one syllable is stressed or emphasized. This syllable is shown in bold. Make sure that you pronounce this syllable louder or with a little more emphasis or your pronunciation won't sound right. Some words even change their meaning when you change the stress. Here's an example:

this	**es**·ta	**ehss**-tah
it is ...	es·**tá**	ehss-**tah**

In some instances, two or three Spanish words are given for an English word. The first word listed is always the word that is most likely to be understood everywhere throughout Latin America. I list additional words if you are likely to hear them and need to understand, or if different words are used in different countries or parts of a country.

③ ***Spanish pronunciation***

This column will always show you how to pronounce the Spanish word or phrase. Even if you can pronounce most words on your own, you can always look at this column to verify your pronunciation.

For some things, Spanish speakers use the same word we use in English, but pronounce it differently. In column 3, I show you how a Spanish speaker pronounces this English word. Often the pronunciation is ***just*** different enough that you might not be understood if you don't give the English word that little Spanish twist.

switch	**switch**	ehss-**weetch**
		swee-cheh

© 2000 Kathy Parsons, Spanish for Cruisers

Nouns (things 🚢 , people 🎩 , concepts ❤)

Every noun (thing, person, concept) is classified as either masculine or feminine. Some classifications make sense. Nouns for male persons and animals are masculine. Nouns for females are feminine. Sometimes you can guess whether a noun is masculine or feminine by its ending. Nouns ending in *o*, *tor*, or *dor* are usually masculine. Nouns ending in *a*, *ción*, or *dad* are usually feminine. Dictionaries usually show an **f** for *feminine* or **m** for *masculine* after the word.

In Spanish there are *four* different words for "the" according to whether a noun is masculine or feminine, singular or plural. These four words are:

the		for...		Example:	
the	**el**	masculine	singular	**el** ta·**ller**	the repair shop
	la	feminine	singular	**la** tien·da	the store
	los	masculine	plural	**los** re·**pues**·tos	the spare parts
	las	feminine	plural	**las** **pie**·zas	the parts

© 2000 Kathy Parsons, Spanish for Cruisers

In this book, a column is displayed to the left of the Spanish noun showing the word for "the" that needs to be pronounced in front of that noun.

①	⇩	②	③
store	la	**tien**da	**tyehn**-dah
repair or workshop	el	ta**ller**	tah-**yehr**
spare parts	los las las	re**pues**tos **pie**zas refac**cio**nes *(Mexico)*	reh-**pwehss**-tohss **pyeh**-sahss reh-fak-**syoh**-nehss

Do I absolutely need to know this?

Not really. If you can, try to use the correct word for "the" shown to the left of the noun. If you are more advanced in Spanish, you can use this information also to place the correct endings on adjectives and words like "this", "that", and "a". The SPANISH FOR CRUISERS series will have a separate lesson book for those who want to learn more about the Spanish language.

© 2000 Kathy Parsons, Spanish for Cruisers

Which Syllable Do You *Stress*?

*Every Spanish word has one syllable which is stressed or emphasized. That syllable should be pronounced a little **louder** and* **stronger** *than the rest of the word. Here are the rules for determining which syllable is stressed:*

If the word ...	stress this syllable:	Example:	English:
...contains an accent mark	the syllable with the **accent mark**	a·**diós** per·**dón** **vál**·vu·la	goodbye excuse me valve
...ends in a **vowel**	the **next to last** syllable	**bue**·no ga·so·li·na	good gasoline
...ends in **n** or **s**	the **next to last** syllable	**gra**·cias tor·**ni**·llos	thank you bolts, screws
...ends in any consonant <u>except</u> **n** or **s**	the **last** syllable	mo·**tor** im·pul·**sor**	motor impeller

*✎ The stressed syllable is always shown in **bold** print in this book. ✎*

Vowels

Each single vowel in Spanish (appearing alone) has only one sound. Once you learn its sound, you can pronounce any word it appears in.

A	E	I	O	U
ah	eh	ee	oh	oo

© 2000 Kathy Parsons, Spanish for Cruisers

Vowel	Sounds like...	as in the English words..	Spanish words	Meaning in English	Pronunciation
a	**ah!**	father	**la** **na**·da	the nothing	**lah** **nah**-dah
e	**eh!**	they	**el** **de**	the *(masculine)* of	**ehl** **deh**
i	**ee!**	kilo	**sí** **sin**	yes without	**see** **seen**
o	**oh!** *(long o)*	no, so	**no** mo·**tor**	no motor, engine	**noh** moh-**tohr**
u	**oo!** *(not yoo!)*	duty, rule	**u**·no **mu**·cho	one many, much	**oo**-noh **moo**-choh
y	**ee!**		**y**	and	**ee**

a, *e*, or *o* together = pronounce each vowel separately (as a separate syllable)

Examples in Spanish	Meaning in English	Pronunciation
co·**rre**·a	belt *(alternator, etc.)*	koh-**rreh**-ah
po·**le**·a	pulley	poh-**leh**-ah
o·**es**·te	west	oh-**ehss**-teh
pro·a	bow of boat	**proh**-ah

© 2000 Kathy Parsons, Spanish for Cruisers

When an i or y (without an accent mark) is combined with (a, e, o, or u), pronounce it as the consonant y:

Vowels	Sounds like...	Examples in Spanish	Meaning in English	Pronunciation
ia	**yah**	**gra**·cias **me**·dia	thank you half	**grah**-syahss **meh**-dyah
ie	**yeh**	**bien** **diez**	well, fine ten	**byehn** **dyehss**
io	**yo**	a·**diós** **cam**·bio	good-bye change	ah-**dyohss** **kahm**-byoh
iu	**yoo**	ciu·**dad**	city	syoo-**dahd**
ai, ay	**eye** (long i)	**ai**·re **hay**	air is there?, there is	**eye**-ray **eye** (h is silent)
ei, ey	**ay**	**seis** a·**cei**·te	six oil	**sayss** ah-**say**-teh
oy, oi	**oy** (as in "boy")	**voy**	I am going	**voy**

However, if the í has an accent mark, pronounce each vowel separately (and stress the í):

Vowels	Sounds like...	Examples in Spanish	Meaning in English	Pronunciation
ía	**ee**-ah	**dí**·a fe·rre·te·**rí**·a	day hardware store	**dee**-ah feh-rreh-teh-**rree**-ah
ío	**ee**-oh	**frí**·o va·**cí**·o	cold empty	**free**-oh vah-**see**-oh

© 2000 Kathy Parsons, Spanish for Cruisers

When a **u** (without an accent mark) is combined with (**a**, **e**, **i**, or **o**), pronounce it as the consonant **w**:

Vowels	Sounds like...	Examples in Spanish	Meaning in English	Pronunciation
ua	wah	¿**cuán**·to?	how much?	**kwahn**-toh
		cuatro	four	kwah-troh
ue	weh	**bue**·no	good	**bweh**-noh
		cuesta	costs	kwehss-tah
au	ow (as in "how")	res·tau·**ran**·te	restaurant	rehss-tow-**rahn**-tay

Except: **u** is silent with **gue, gui, que, qui**

Vowels	Sounds like...	Examples in Spanish	Meaning in English	Pronunciation
gue	**gh**eh (as in "get")	man·**gue**·ra	hose	mahn-**gheh**-rah
gui	**gh**ee (as in "geek")	**guí**·a	guide	**ghee**-ah
que	keh (as in "kay")	**tan**·que	tank	**tahn**-keh
qui	kee (as in "key")	**má**·qui·na	machine	**mah**-kee-nah
		qui·lla	keel	**kee**-yah

Read my lips! *Speak slowly and distinctly, syllable-by-syllable. Exaggerate a little, producing **nice, big** Spanish vowel sounds. Don't try to win any speed contests. You will find that people understand you much better when you take it slow-and-easy!*

© 2000 Kathy Parsons, Spanish for Cruisers

Most of the consonants are pronounced the same (or almost the same) in English and Spanish. But note that an L by itself is pronounced as in English, but a double L is pronounced like y. Also watch out for these consonants which tend to give us trouble: g (when followed by e or i), h, j, q, s, and z.

Vowel	Sounds like...	as in the English words..	Spanish words	Meaning in English	Pronunciation
b	*same as English*				
c + *anything but* **e, i**	**k**	cat	**ca**·ble	cable, wire	**kah**-bleh
c + **e, i**	**s**	city	**cin**·co a·**cei**·te	five oil	**seen**-koh ah-**say**-teh
ch	*same as English*	church	**o**·cho **mu**·cho	eight many, much	**oh**-choh **moo**-choh
d, f	*same as English*				
g + *anything but* **e, i**	**g**	go	ga·so·li·na **gra**·cias	gasoline thank you	gah-soh-**lee**-nah **grah**-syahss
g + **e, i**	**h**		a·**gen**·te	agent	ah-**hehn**-teh
h	***always silent!*** *Do not pronounce!*		**ho**·la **hoy**	hello today	**oh**-lah **oy**
j	**h**	hot	**ba**·jo bu·**jí**·a	low spark plug	**bah**-hoh boo-**hee**-ah
k	*same as English*				
l	*same as English*				

© 2000 Kathy Parsons, Spanish for Cruisers

Vowel	Sounds like...	as in the English words..	Spanish words	Meaning in English	Pronunciation
ll	**y**	yes	tor·ti·lla lla·ve	tortilla key, wrench	tohr-**tee**-yah **yah**-veh
m, n	*same as English*				
ñ	**ny**	canyon	ma·**ña**·na	tomorrow, morning	mah-**nyah**-nah
p	*same as English*				
qu	**k** *(not kw!)*		**qué** a·**quí**	what? here	**keh** ah-**kee**
r	*same as English*				
rr	*trill that r!*		ce·**rra**·do	closed	seh-**rrah**-doh
s	**s** *(not z!)*	see	fu·**si**·ble	fuse	foo-**see**-bleh
t	*same as English*				
v	**v** *or* **b** *(depends on location & speaker)*		ve·**le**·ro **vál**·vu·la	sailboat valve	veh-**leh**-roh **vahl**-voo-lah
w	*seldom seen*				
x *(most words)*	*same as English*		**ta**·xi	taxi	**tah**-ksee
x *(Mayan words)*	**h**	hot	**Mé**·xi·co	Mexico	**Meh**-hee-koh
y	*same as English*	yes	**yo** in·yec·**tor**	I injector	**yoh** een-yehk-**tohr**
z	**s** *(not z!)*	see	**zinc** **luz**	zinc light, electricity	**seenk** **looss** **

** The pronunciation for **s** and **z** is shown as **ss** at the end of a syllable, to discourage our natural tendency to pronounce **s** and **z** as **zz**.

© 2000 Kathy Parsons, Spanish for Cruisers

Here are some good reasons to learn the alphabet:
- ✓ *When you communicate over the radio, you will often be asked to spell the name of your boat*
- ✓ *Many common terms such as VHF, GPS, RPM, PSI, and LCD are referred to by their initials. You need to know the alphabet to pronounce these correctly.*
- ✓ *Reciting the alphabet aloud (like we did as kids), helps you memorize the sound of each letter.*

Letter	Name	Pronunciation
a	a	ah
b	be (gran·de)	beh (grahn-deh)
c	ce	seh
ch	che	cheh
d	de	deh
e	e	eh
f	e·fe	eh-feh
g	ge	heh
h	a·che	ah-cheh
i	i	ee
j	jo·ta	hoh-tah
k	ka	kah
l	e·le	eh-leh
ll	e·lle	eh-yeh
m	e·me	eh-meh

Letter	Name	Pronunciation
n	e·ne	eh-neh
ñ	e·ñe	eh-nyeh
o	o	oh
p	pe	peh
q	cu	koo
r	e·re	eh-reh
rr	e·rre (do·ble e·re)	eh-rrreh
s	e·se	eh-seh
t	te	teh
u	u	oo
v	ve (pe·que·ño)	veh peh-keh-nyoh
w	do·ble u	doh-bleh oo
x	e·quis	eh-keess
y	i·grie·ga	ee-gryeh-gah
z	ze·ta	seh-tah

© 2000 Kathy Parsons, Spanish for Cruisers

Questions and Answers		
How is it written (spelled)?	¿Cómo se escribe?	Koh-moh seh ehss-kree-beh ?
It is written a – b - c ...	Se escribe a - b - c ...	Seh ehss-kree-beh ...
It is spelled a - b - c ...	Se deletrea a - b - c ...	Seh deh-leh-treh-ah ...
Write it, please.	Escríbalo, por favor.	Ehss-kree-bah-loh, pohr fah-vohr.
My last name is written (spelled) ...	Mi apellido se escribe ...	Mee ah-peh-yee-doh seh ehss-kree-beh ...
My first name is written (spelled) ...	Mi nombre se escribe ...	Mee nohm-breh seh ehss-kree-beh ...
The name of the boat is written (spelled) ...	El nombre del barco se escribe ...	Ehl nohm-breh dehl bahr-koh seh ehss-kree-beh ...

Some common initials		
VHF (radio)	VHF	veh ah-cheh eh-feh
SSB (radio)	SSB	eh-seh eh-seh beh
GPS (radio)	GPS	heh peh eh-seh
RPM	RPM (revolutions per minute)	eh-reh peh eh-meh
PSI	PSI (pounds per square inch)	peh es-seh ee
R-12	R-12	eh-reh doh-seh

© 2000 Kathy Parsons, Spanish for Cruisers

Greetings

Good morning	**Bue**nos **dí**as	Bweh-nohss dee-ahss
Good afternoon	**Bue**nas **tar**des	Bweh-nahss tahr-dehss
Good evening *(after dark)*	**Bue**nas **no**ches	Bweh-nahss noh-chehss

Good-byes

Until later	**Has**ta **lue**go	Ahss-tah lweh-goh
Until tomorrow	**Has**ta ma**ña**na	Ahss-tah mah-nyah-nah
Goodbye	A·**diós**	Ah-dyohss
Ciao, goodbye *(Venezuela)*	**Cha**o	Chah-oh (chow)
See you!	¡**Nos ve**mos!	Nohss veh-mohss
See you *Monday (Tuesday, etc..)*	**Nos ve**mos *el lu*nes *(martes..)*	Nohss veh-mohss *ehl loo-nehss ...*
Good trip	**Buen via**je	Bwehn vyah-heh

Hasta mañana, Nos vemos el lunes, etc. are handy ways to say goodbye. They remind the person you are talking to that you have made an agreement to meet them again or to pick up your job on a certain day or at a certain time.

Please and Thank you

Please	**Por** fa·**vor**	Por fah-vohr
Thank you	**Gra**·cias	Grah-syahss
Many thanks	**Mu**chas **gra**·cias	Moo-chahss grah-syahss
You're welcome	**De na**da	Deh nah-dah
You're welcome *(clerks say this)*	**Pa**·ra ser·**vir**·le	Pah-rah sehr-veer-leh

© 2000 Kathy Parsons, Spanish for Cruisers

At your service *(clerks say this)*	**A su or**·den	*Ah soo ohr-dehn*
Yes? Your order? *(Mexico only)*	¿**Man**·de?	**Mahn**-deh?

Yes

Yes	**Sí**	**See**
OK *or* It's fine.	Es**tá bien**.	Ehss-**tah byehn**. *(ehss-tah,* not *ehss-tah!)*
Of course!	¡**Có**·mo **no**!	**Koh**-moh **noh!**
Sure	**Cla**·ro	**Klah**-roh
No problem! *(there is no problem)*	**No hay** pro·**ble**·ma!	No eye pro-**bleh**-mah!
Good	**Bue**·no	**Bweh**-noh

No

No	**No**	**Noh**
Maybe	**Tal vez**	**Tahl vehss**
I don't know ... (yet)	**No sé** ... (to·da·**ví**·a)	**Noh seh** ... (toh-dah-**vee**-ah)
I can't.	**No pue**·do	**Noh pweh**-doh.
Not today	**Hoy no**	**Oy noh**
It is not possible.	**No es** po·**si**·ble.	**Noh ehss** poh-**see**-bleh.
There isn't any.	**No hay**.	**Noh eye**.
I'm only looking.	**So**·lo es**toy** mi·**ran**·do.	**Soh**-loh ehss-**toy** mee-**rahn**-doh.
I'll come back later.	**Ven**·go **lue**·go.	**Vehn**-goh **lweh**-goh.

© 2000 Kathy Parsons, Spanish for Cruisers

Excuse me...

Excuse me *(general purpose)*	Per**dón**	Pehr-**dohn**
Excuse me *(with your permission)* *(used when you squeeze by someone or when you need someone to let you pass)*	**Con** per**mi**so	**Kohn** pehr-**mee**-soh
I'm sorry	**Lo sien**to	Loh **syehn**-toh

I don't understand...

I don't understand	**No** com**pren**do	Noh kohm-**prehn**-doh
Again, please	O·tra **vez, por** fa·**vor**	Oh-trah **vehss, pohr** fah-**vohr**
Repeat, please	Re·**pi**·ta, **por** fa·**vor**	Reh-**pee**-tah, **pohr** fah-**vohr**
More slowly, please	**Más** des·**pa**·cio, **por** fa·**vor**	**Mahss** dehss-pah-syoh, ...
Write it down, please	Es·**crí**·ba·lo, **por** fa·**vor**	Ehss-**kree**-bah-loh, ...
One moment, please	**Un** mo·**men**·to, **por** fa·**vor**	Oon moh-**mehn**-toh, ...
What is this?	¿**Qué es es**·to?	Keh ehss ehss-toh?
What is this called?	¿**Có**·mo **se lla**·ma **es**·to?	Koh-moh **seh yah**-mah **ehss**-toh?

How are you?

How are you? *("you" is implied)*	¿**Có**·mo es·**tá**?	Koh-moh ehss-**tah**?
Fine, thank you.	**Bien, gra**·cias.	Byehn **grah**-syahss.
And you? *(polite)*	¿**Y** us·**ted**?	Ee ooss-**tehd**?

© 2000 Kathy Parsons, Spanish for Cruisers

Introductions		
My name is ... *(I call myself)*	**Me lla**mo ... *(name)*	**Meh yah**-moh ...
I'm ... *(name)*	**Soy** ... *(name)*	**Soy** ...
I'm American. *(male speaking)*	**Soy** norteameri**ca**no.	**Soy nohr**-teh-ah-meh-ree-**kah**-noh.
I'm American. *(female speaking)*	**Soy** norteameri**ca**na.	**Soy nohr**-teh-ah-meh-ree-**kah**-nah.
We are American.	**So**mos norteameri**ca**nos.	**Soh**-mohss **nohr**-teh-ah-meh-ree-**kah**-nohss.
I am from the United States.	**Soy de los** Esta·dos U·ni·dos.	**Soy deh lohss** Ehss-**tah**-dohss Oo-**nee**-dohss.
We are from Canada.	**So**mos **de** Cana**dá**.	**Soh**-mohss **deh** Kah-nah-**dah**.
My sailboat is ... *(name)*	**Mi** ve·le·ro **es** ... *(name)*	**Mee** veh-**leh**-roh **ehss** ...
My boat is ... *(name)*	**Mi bar**·co **es** ... *(name)*	**Mee bahr**-koh **ehss** ...
What's your name? *(How are you called?)*	¿**Có**mo **se lla**ma?	**Koh**-moh **seh yah**-mah?
Pleased to meet you.	**Mu**·cho **gus**·to.	**Moo**-choh **gooss**-toh.

It's not surprising that Latin Americans often refer to those of us from the USA as "gringos" when you consider the alternative! People from the United States usually call themselves "Americans". However, Spanish speakers consider anyone who lives in North, Central or South America an "americano". Thus, citizens of the United States are "norteamericanos" (northamericans) and that is quite a mouthful!

© 2000 Kathy Parsons, Spanish for Cruisers

What, Who, How, Why ...?		
What is ...? *or* What is it?	¿**Qué es** ...?	Keh ehss ... ?
Which is ...?	¿**Cuál es** ...?	Kwahl ehss ... ?
Who is ...? *or* Who is it?	¿**Quién es** ...?	Kyehn ehss ... ?
How ...?	¿**Có**·mo ...?	Koh-moh ... ?
Why ...?	¿**Por qué** ...?	Pohr keh ... ?

Where ...?		
Where is ...?	¿**Dón**·de es·**tá** ...?	Dohn-deh ehss-**tah** ... ?
Where is there ...?	¿**Dón**·de **hay** ...?	Dohn-deh **eye** ... ?

When ...?		
When ...?	¿**Cuán**·do ...?	Kwahn-doh ... ?
At what time ...?	¿**A qué ho**·ra ...?	Ah keh oh-rah ... ?
How long ...?	¿**Cuán**·to **tiem**·po?	Kwahn-toh **tyehm**-poh ... ?

How much ...?		
How much ...?	¿**Cuán**·to ...?	Kwahn-toh ... ?
How much does it cost?	¿**Cuán**·to **cues**·ta?	Kwahn-toh **kwehss**-tah?
How many ...?	¿**Cuán**·tos ...?	Kwahn-tohss ... ?

© 2000 Kathy Parsons, Spanish for Cruisers

Do you have ...?		
Is there ...? or Are there ...?	¿**Hay** ...? (very common, very useful!)	**Eye** ...?
Do you have ...?	¿**Tie**ne ...?	**Tyeh**-neh ...?

... need ...?		
Do I need ...?	¿Ne·ce·si·to ...?	Neh-seh-**see**-toh ...?
Do you need ...?	¿Ne·ce·si·ta us**ted** ...? *	Neh-seh-**see**-tah ooss-**tehd** ...?
Do you want ...?	¿**Quie**·re us**ted** ...? *	**Kyeh**-reh ooss-**tehd** ...?
Can you ...?	¿**Pue**·de us**ted** ...? *	**Pweh**-deh ooss-**tehd** ... ?

** You can omit **usted** since it will generally be understood from the context of your question.*

Is it ...?		
Is it OK (fine)?	¿Es**tá bien**?	Ehss-**tah byehn**?
Is it possible ...?	¿**Es** po·si·ble ...?	**Ehss** poh-**see**-bleh ...?
Is it ...? (*when asking about something's identity or characteristics*)	¿**Es** ...?	**Ehss** ...?
is it ...? (*when asking about something's location or status*)	¿Es**tá** ...?	Ehss-**tah** ...?

By the way ...

Spanish has 2 different sets of words for is and are:
*está and están = when describing something's **temporary status** or **location**.*
*es and son = when describing something's **identity** or **permanent characteristics**.*

But don't sweat it – you will usually be understood whichever you use!

© 2000 Kathy Parsons, Spanish for Cruisers

You can make any sentence negative by placing **no** before the verb.

It is ...		
It is ... (*when describing something's identity or characteristics*)	**Es** ...	**Ehss** ...
It is ... (*when describing something's location or status*)	Es·**tá** ...	Ehss-**tah** ... (*ehss-TAH, <u>not</u> ehss-tah!*)
It is located at/in ...	Es·**tá** **en** ...	Ehss-**tah** **ehn** ...
It isn't here. He isn't here.	**No** es·tá.	**Noh** ehss-tah.
It costs ...		
It costs ...	**Cues**·ta ...	**Kwehss**-tah ...
There is ...		
There is ... *or* There are ...	**Hay** ... (*very common, very useful!*)	**Eye** ...
There isn't any.	**No hay** ... (*very common, very useful!*)	**Noh eye**.
... need ...		
I need ...	Ne·ce·**si**·to ...	Neh-seh-**see**-toh ...
I don't need ...	**No** ne·ce·**si**·to ...	**Noh** neh-seh-**see**-toh ...
You need ...	Ne·ce·**si**·ta ... Us·**ted** ne·ce·**si**·ta ... *	Neh-seh-**see**-tah ... Ooss-**tehd** neh-seh-**see**-tah ...
We need ...	Ne·ce·**si·ta**·mos ...	Neh-seh-see-**tah**-mohss ...

** You can omit **Usted** since it will generally be understood from the context of your sentence.*

© 2000 Kathy Parsons, Spanish for Cruisers

... have ...		
I have ...	**Ten**go ...	**Tehn**-goh ...
I don't have ...	**No ten**go ...	No tehn-goh ...
It has ...	**Tie**ne ...	**Tyeh**-neh ...
We have ...	Te**ne**mos ...	Teh-**neh**-mohss ...

... want ...		
I want ...	**Quie**ro ...	**Kyeh**-roh ...
I don't want ...	**No quie**ro ...	**Noh kyeh**-roh ...
We want ...	Que**re**mos ...	Keh-**reh**-mohss ...

By the way ...

In Spanish, the same verb construction is used for statements and questions. For example:
   Es means either "**It is...**" or "**Is It..?**" depending on your tone of voice.
   Ne·ce·si·to means either "**I need...**" or "**Do I need...?**" depending on your tone of voice.
Furthermore, the pronouns **I, you, he, she, it, we, they** are often omitted in Spanish because the ending of the verb usually tells you who is speaking:
   The **o** ending on Necesito... means "**I need...**"
   The **a** ending on Necesita... can mean either "*You need*", "*He needs*", "*She needs*" or "*It needs*". So if it is not clear from the context or your tone of voice, you can add us**ted** ("*you*") for clarity:
      Do you need ...? :   ¿ Ne·ce·si·ta ...? ...or... ¿ Ne·ce·si·ta us**ted**...?

© 2000 Kathy Parsons, Spanish for Cruisers

SENTENCE STARTERS can be used with ACTION PHRASES to describe what you need to do and want to do. QUESTION STARTERS can be used with ACTION PHRASES to make requests and ask about the work that needs to be performed. They are used throughout this book to communicate with mechanics, clerks, and repairmen.

You will find ACTION PHRASES in the TROUBLESHOOTING and MAINTENANCE sections throughout this book.

You may combine virtually any sentence or question starter and action phrase. Don't worry about the (to) shown in the English. If it is required in the Spanish, it will have already been placed in the appropriate place in the Spanish sentence starter. Here are some examples:

I need to + fill the tank.	Ne·ce·si·to + lle·**nar el tan**·que.
Can you + check the alternator?	¿**Pue**·de + re·vi·**sar el** al·ter·na·**dor**?
How much does it cost to + fix the outboard?	¿**Cuán**·to **cues**·ta + re·pa·**rar la** fue·ra·**bor**·da?
Do I need to + pull the motor?	¿Ne·ce·si·to + sa·**car el** mo·**tor**?

Sentence starters		
I need (to) ...	Ne·ce·**si**·to ...	Neh-seh-**see**-toh ...
I want (to) ...	**Quie**·ro ...	**Kyeh**-roh ...
I am going to ...	**Voy a** ...	**Voy ah** ...
I can ...	**Pue**·do ...	**Pweh**-doh ...
I can't ...	**No pue**·do ...	**Noh pweh**-doh ...
You need (to) ...	Ne·ce·**si**·ta ...	Neh-seh-**see**-tah ...
	Us·**ted** ne·ce·**si**·ta ...	Oo-**stehd** neh-seh-**see**-tah ...
You don't need (to) ...	**No** ne·ce·**si**·ta ...	**Noh** neh-seh-**see**-tah ...
	Us·**ted no** ne·ce·**si**·ta ...	Ooss-**tehd noh** neh-seh-**see**-tah ...

© 2000 Kathy Parsons, Spanish for Cruisers

You can ...	**Pue**de ... Us**ted pue**de ...	**Pweh**-deh ... Ooss-**tehd pweh**-deh ...
It needs (to) ...	Ne·ce·**si**·ta ...	Neh-seh-**see**-tah ...
We need (to) ...	Ne·ce·si·**ta**·mos ...	Neh-seh-see-**tah**-mohss ...
We want (to) ...	Que·**re**·mos ...	Keh-**reh**-mohss ...
We are going to ...	**Va**·mos **a** ...	**Vah**-mohss **ah** ...
We can ...	Po·**de**·mos ...	Poh-**deh**-mohss ...
We can't ...	**No** po·**de**·mos ...	**Noh** poh-**deh**-mohss ...

Question starters

Do I need to ...?	¿Ne·ce·**si**·to ...?	Neh-seh-**see**-toh ...?
Do you need to ...?	¿Ne·ce·**si**·ta ...? ¿Ne·ce·**si**·ta us·**ted**...?	Neh-seh-**see**-tah ...? Neh-seh-**see**-tah ooss-**tehd**...?
Do you want to ...?	¿ **Quie**·re ...? ¿ **Quie**·re us·**ted**...?	**Kyeh**-reh ...? **Kyeh**-reh ooss-**tehd**...?
Can you ...?	¿**Pue**·de ...?	**Pweh**-deh ...?
Are you going to ...?	¿**Va a** ...?	**Vah ah** ...?
Do we need to ...?	¿Ne·ce·si·**ta**·mos ...?	Neh-seh-see-**tah**-mohss ...?
Should I ...? (Must I ...?)	¿**De**·bo ... ?	**Deh**-boh ... ?
How much does it cost to ...?	¿**Cuán**·to **cues**·ta ...?	**Kwahn**-toh **kwehss**-tah ...?
How much time do you need to ..?	¿**Cuán**·to **tiem**·po ne·ce·si·ta **pa**·ra ...?	**Kwahn**-toh **tyehm**-poh neh-seh-**see**-tah **pah**-rah ...?

© 2000 Kathy Parsons, Spanish for Cruisers

These are those little words that hold your sentences together. Highlight the ones you want to learn.

a	**un** (masc.)	**oon**
	una (fem.)	**oo-nah**
all	**to**do	**toh-doh**
also, too	tam**bién**	tahm-**byehn**
and	**y**	**ee**
at ...*(place)*	**en**	**ehn**
at ...*(time)*	**a**	**ah**
because	**por**que	**pohr**-keh
between	**en**·tre	**ehn**-treh
but	**pe**·ro	**peh**-roh
by	**por**	**pohr**
each, every	**ca**·da	**kah**-dah
for	**pa**·ra	**pah**-rah
	por	**pohr**
here	a·**quí**	ah-**kee**
if	**si**	**see**
in	**en**	**ehn**
no, not	**no**	**noh**
of, from	**de**	**deh**
on	**en**	**ehn**
or	**o**	**oh**
per	**por**	**pohr**

*Use **un** with masculine nouns (nouns with **el** in the second column), **una** with feminine nouns (nouns with **la** in the second column). See Chapter 1 pages 7-8 for more on masculine and feminine nouns.*

*When **for** means "intended for or to be used with", use **para**. Beyond that, don't fret it!*

*si (if) is pronounced the same as **sí** (yes)*

*In English, we often make a sentence negative by placing **do not** or **does not** before the verb. In Spanish, just place **no** before the verb.*

*In English, we often use a noun before another noun to describe it: **credit card**, **travelers check**, **oil pressure**. In Spanish you say: card **of credit** (tarjeta **de crédito**), check **of traveler** (cheque **de viajero**), pressure **of oil** (presión **de aceite**)*

© 2000 Kathy Parsons, Spanish for Cruisers

that	e·so	eh-soh
there	a·llá	ah-**yah**
	a·llí	ah-**yee**
this	es·to	ehss-toh
to	**a**	ah
toward	**ha**·cia	ah-syah
until	**has**·ta	ahss-tah
with	**con**	kohn
without	**sin**	seen

I	**yo**	yoh
you	us·**ted**	ooss-**tehd**
you *(plural)*	us·**te**·des	ooss-**teh**-dehss
we	no·**so**·tros	noh-**soh**-trohss
they	e·llos	eh-yohss
he	**él**	ehl
she	e·lla	eh-yah
my	**mi**	mee
your, her, his, their	**su**	soo
our	**nues**·tro	nwehss-troh

That can be **ese, esa,** or **eso** depending on whether you're referring to a masculine, feminine or unknown noun.

Use either **allí** or **allá** for **there**. But where we say **there is, there are, is there ...?,** and **are there ...?** to say or ask if something exists, Spanish just uses the one word **hay.** See pgs. 22, 23, and 33 for uses of **hay.**

This can be **este, esta,** or **esto** depending on whether you're referring to a masculine, feminine or unknown noun. Always stress the **first** syllable – **EHSS-**toh!

I, you, he, she, we, and *they* are often omitted from Spanish sentences. They are usually redundant since the ending on the verb will tell you who is being referred to.

Usted is the polite or formal word for **you** and is used throughout this book. There is another word for **you (tú),** but it is used only when you are on a first name basis with a person.

There really isn't a word for **it** (as the subject of a sentence) in Spanish. *It* is implied by the verb ending and the context of the sentence.

© 2000 Kathy Parsons, Spanish for Cruisers

Handy hint for understanding numbers ...

*When anyone says a number to you in Spanish, **immediately** (before you translate the number in your head), say the number you heard aloud in Spanish. This way, the person can confirm that you heard the number accurately, or correct you if you got it wrong.*

Once you've confirmed that you correctly heard the number, repeat it over and over in your head until you can translate the number.

This will save you lots of misunderstandings since certain numbers such as 60, 70, and 100 sound very similar.

1	u·no	oo-noh		11	on·ce	ohn-seh
2	dos	dohss		12	do·ce	doh-seh
3	tres	trehss		13	tre·ce	treh-seh
4	cua·tro	kwah-troh		14	ca·tor·ce	kah-**tohr**-seh
5	cin·co	seen-koh		15	quin·ce	keen-seh
6	seis	sayss		16	diez y seis	dyehss ee sayss
7	sie·te	syeh-teh		17	diez y sie·te	dyehss ee syeh-teh
8	o·cho	oh-choh		18	diez y o·cho	dyehss ee oh-choh
9	nue·ve	nweh-veh		19	diez y nue·ve	dyehss ee nweh-veh
10	diez	dyehss				

© 2000 Kathy Parsons, Spanish for Cruisers

20	**vein**·te	**vayn**-teh
21	vein·ti·**u**·no	vayn-tee-**oo**-noh
22	vein·ti·**dós**	vayn-tee-**dohss**
23	vein·ti·**trés**	vayn-tee-**trehss**
24	vein·ti·**cua**·tro	vayn-tee-**kwah**-troh
25	vein·ti·**cin**·co	vayn-tee-**seen**-koh
26	vein·ti·**séis**	vayn-tee-**sayss**
27	vein·ti·**sie**·te	vayn-tee-**syeh**-teh
28	vein·ti·o·cho	vayn-tee-**oh**-choh
29	vein·ti·**nue**·ve	vayn-tee-**nweh**-veh

30	**trein**·ta	**trayn**-tah
31	**trein**·ta **y** **u**·no	**trayn**-tah **ee** **oo**-noh
32	**trein**·ta **y** dos	**trayn**-tah **ee** dohss
33	**trein**·ta **y** tres	**trayn**-tah **ee** trehss

40	cua·**ren**·ta	kwah-**rehn**-tah
41	cua·**ren**·ta **y** **u**·no	kwah-**rehn**-tah **ee** **oo**-noh
42	cua·**ren**·ta **y** dos	kwah-**rehn**-tah **ee** dohss

50	cin·**cuen**·ta	seen-**kwehn**-tah
51	cin·**cuen**·ta **y** **u**·no	seen-**kwehn**-tah **ee** **oo**-noh
52	cin·**cuen**·ta **y** dos	seen-**kwehn**-tah **ee** dohss

60	se·**sen**·ta	seh-**sehn**-tah
61	se·**sen**·ta **y** **u**·no	seh-**sehn**-tah **ee** **oo**-noh
62	se·**sen**·ta **y** dos	seh-**sehn**-tah **ee** dohss

70	se·**ten**·ta	seh-**tehn**-tah
71	se·**ten**·ta **y** **u**·no	seh-**tehn**-tah **ee** **oo**-noh
72	se·**ten**·ta **y** dos	seh-**tehn**-tah **ee** dohss

80	o·**chen**·ta	oh-**chehn**-tah
81	o·**chen**·ta **y** **u**·no	oh-**chehn**-tah **ee** **oo**-noh
82	o·**chen**·ta **y** dos	oh-**chehn**-tah **ee** dohss

90	no·**ven**·ta	noh-**vehn**-tah
91	no·**ven**·ta **y** **u**·no	noh-**vehn**-tah **ee** **oo**-noh
92	no·**ven**·ta **y** dos	noh-**vehn**-tah **ee** dohss

© 2000 Kathy Parsons, Spanish for Cruisers

100	**cien**	syehn
101	**cien**to **u**no	**syehn**-toh **oo**-noh
102	**cien**to **dos**	**syehn**-toh **dohss**
103	**cien**to **tres**	**syehn**-toh **trehss**

200	dos**cien**tos	dohss-**syehn**-tohss
201	dos**cien**tos **u**no	dohss-**syehn**-tohss oo-noh
300	tres**cien**tos	trehss-**syehn**-tohss
400	cua·tro**cien**tos	kwah-troh-**syehn**-tohss
500	qui**nien**tos	kee-**nyehn**-tohss
600	seis**cien**tos	sayss-**syehn**-tohss
700	se·te**cien**tos	seh-teh-**syehn**-tohss
800	o·cho**cien**tos	oh-choh-**syehn**-tohss
900	no·ve**cien**tos	no-veh-**syehn**-tohss

Practice counting aloud in Spanish. It will help you learn the numbers and will train your mouth to produce the Spanish sounds more easily.

1000	**mil**	meel
1999	**mil** no·ve**cien**tos no·**ven**ta y **nue**ve	meel noh-veh-**syehn**-tohss noh-**vehn**-tah ee nweh-veh
2000	**dos mil**	**dohss** meel
3000	**tres mil**	**trehss** meel
10,000	**diez mil**	**dyehss** meel
100,000	**cien mil**	**syehn** meel
1 million	**un** mi**llón**	oon mee-**yohn**

0	**ce**ro	**seh**-roh
1.2	**u**no **pun**to **dos**	oo-noh **poon**-toh **dohss**
2 ½	**dos** y **me**dio	**dohss** y meh-**dyoh**

½	**me**dio	meh-**dyoh**
¼	**un cuar**to	oon **kwahr**-toh
¾	**tres cuar**tos	**trehss kwahr**-tohss
1/8	**un** oc**ta**vo	oon ohk-**tah**-voh
1/16	**un** die·ci·seis·a·vo	oon dyeh-see-sayss-ah-voh

© 2000 Kathy Parsons, Spanish for Cruisers

Country		Currency *(singular)*	Pronunciation	Currency *(plural)*	Pronunciation
Argentina, Chile, Colombia, Cuba, Dominican Republic, Mexico, Uruguay	el	**pe**·so	**peh**-soh	**pe**·sos	**peh**-sohss
Costa Rica	el	co·**lón**	koh-**lohn**	co·**lo**·nes	koh-**loh**-nehss
Ecuador	el	**su**·cre	**soo**-kreh	**su**·cres	**soo**-krehss
El Salvador	el	co·**lón**	koh-**lohn**	co·**lo**·nes	koh-**loh**-nehss
Guatemala	el	quet·**zal**	keht-**sahl**	quet·**za**·les	keht-**sah**-lehss
Honduras	la	lem·**pi**·ra	lehm-**pee**-rah	lem·**pi**·ras	lehm-**pee**-rahss
Nicaragua	la	**cór**·do·ba	**kohr**-doh-bah	**cór**·do·bas	**kohr**-doh-bahss
Panama	el	**dó**·lar (US)	**doh**-lahr	**dó**·la·res	**doh**-lah-rehss
	la	bal·**bo**·a	bahl-**boh**-ah	bal·**bo**·as	bahl-**boh**-ahss
Peru	el	**sol**	**sohl**	**so**·les	**soh**-lehss
Puerto Rico	el	**dó**·lar *(also pe·so)*	**doh**-lahr	**dó**·la·res	**doh**-lah-rehss
Venezuela	el	bo·**lí**·var	boh-**lee**-vahr	bo·**lí**·va·res	boh-**lee**-vah-rehss
cent	el	cen·**ta**·vo	sehn-**tah**-voh	cen·**ta**·vos	sehn-**tah**-vohss
money	el	di·**ne**·ro	dee-**neh**-roh		
cash	el	e·fec·**ti**·vo	eh-fehk-**tee**-voh		

Several currencies above have accent marks: Be careful with their pronunciation:
*dó·lar is pronounced **doh**-lahr   (not doh-**lahr**!)*
*bo·lí·var is pronounced boh-**lee**-vahr (not boh-lee-**vahr**!)*

© 2000 Kathy Parsons, Spanish for Cruisers

Always say "Buenos Días" or "Buenas Tardes" to the clerk when you enter a store.
Always say "Gracias" or "Hasta Luego" when you leave.

The clerk might ask:			
	What would you like (desire)?	¿Qué desea?	Keh deh-seh-ah?
	Can I help you?	¿Puedo ayudarle?	Pweh-doh ah-yoo-dahr-leh?
	Yes? *(Mexico only)*	¿Mande?	Mahn-deh?

Do you have...?

Do you have ...?	¿Tiene ...?	Tyeh-neh ...?
Is there ...?	¿Hay ...?	Eye ...?
How many do you have?	¿Cuántos tiene?	Kwahn-tohss tyeh-neh?
I need ...	Necesito ...	Neh-seh-see-toh ...
I want ...	Quiero ...	Kyeh-roh ...
Do you have something cheaper?	¿Tiene algo más barato?	Tyeh-neh ahl-goh mahss bah-rah-toh?
Can I see it?	¿Puedo verlo?	Pweh-doh vehr-loh?

The clerk might respond:			
	There isn't any.	No hay.	Noh eye.
	Yes, there is.	Sí, hay.	See, eye.
	Take it. *(buy it...)*	Llévalo.	Yeh-vah-loh.
	Something else?	¿Algo más?	Ahl-goh mahss?

Will you get more?

Are you going to receive more?	¿Va a recibir más?	Vah ah reh-see-beer mahss?

© 2000 Kathy Parsons, Spanish for Cruisers

When are you going to receive more?	¿**Cuán**do **va a** reci**bir más** ...?	Kwahn-doh **vah ah** reh-see-**beer mahss**?
Can you order ...?	¿**Pue**de or·de**nar** ...?	Pweh-deh ohr-deh-**nahr** ...?
Where can I buy...?	¿**Dón**de **pue**do com**prar** ...?	Dohn-deh **pweh**-doh kohm-**prahr** ...?
...like this but ...	...**co**mo **es**to **pe**ro ...	...koh-moh **ehss**-toh **peh**-roh ...

How much does it cost?		
How much does it cost?	¿**Cuán**to **cues**ta?	Kwahn-toh **kwehss**-tah?
How much does ... cost ?	¿**Cuan**to **cues**ta ...?	Kwahn-toh **kwehss**-tah ... ?

I'll take it...		
It's fine. OK.	Es**tá bien**.	Ehss-tah **byehn**.
That's all.	**Es to**do.	Ehss **toh**-doh.
I'll take it.	**Lo lle**vo.	Loh **yeh**-voh.
I only need one.	**So**lo ne·ce·si·to **u**no.	Soh-loh neh-seh-**see**-toh **oo**-noh.

No, Thanks ...		
I'm only looking.	**So**lo es**toy** mi**ran**do.	Soh-loh ehss-**toy** mee-**rahn**-doh.
I don't know yet.	**No sé** to·da**ví**a.	Noh seh toh-dah-**vee**-ah.
It's very expensive.	**Es muy ca**ro.	Ehss mwee kah-roh.
I'll come (back) later.	**Ven**go **lue**go	Vehn-goh **lweh**-goh.

The clerk might say:	At your service. *(You're welcome.)*	**A su or**den.	**Ah soo ohr**-dehn.
	In order to serve you *(You're welcome.)*	**Pa**ra ser**vir**le.	**Pah**-rah sehr-**veer**-leh.

© 2000 Kathy Parsons, Spanish for Cruisers

Can I pay with ...?

Can I pay with …	¿Puedo pagar con …	Pweh-doh pah-gahr kohn …
… credit card?	… tarjeta de crédito?	… tahr-heh-tah deh creh-dee-toh?
… travelers check?	… cheque de viajero?	… cheh-keh deh vyah-heh-roh?
Is it enough?	¿Es suficiente?	Ehss soo-fee-syehn-teh?
Where do I need to pay?	¿Dónde necesito pagar?	Dohn-deh neh-seh-see-toh pah-gahr?

What you pay with

money	el	dinero	dee-neh-roh
cash	el	efectivo	eh-fehk-tee-voh
dollars	los	dólares	doh-lah-rehss
credit card	la	tarjeta de crédito	tahr-heh-tah deh kreh-dee-toh
VISA card	la	tarjeta VISA	tahr-heh-tah vee-sah
travelers check	el	cheque de viajero	cheh-keh deh vyah-heh-roh

Bills and Receipts

invoice, bill in store	la	factura	fahk-too-rah
bill or check in restaurant	la	cuenta	kwehn-tah
receipt	el	recibo	reh-see-boh
estimate	el	presupuesto	preh-soo-pwehss-toh
copy	la	copia	koh-pyah

© 2000 Kathy Parsons, Spanish for Cruisers

Prices and Charges			
deposit	el	de·**pó**·si·to	deh-**poh**-see-toh
discount	el	des·**cuen**·to	dehss-**kwehn**-toh
expense	el	**gas**·to	**gahss**-toh
free of charge		**gra**·tis	**grah**-teess
job, work	el	tra·**ba**·jo	trah-**bah**-hoh
labor	la	**ma**·no **de o**·bra	**mah**-noh **deh oh**-brah
materials	los	ma·te·**ria**·les	mah-teh-**ryah**-lehss
maximum	el	**má**·xi·mo	**mah**-ksee-moh
minimum	el	**mí**·ni·mo	**mee**-nee-moh
price	el	**pre**·cio	**preh**-syoh
rate, price, fare	la	ta·**ri**·fa	tah-**ree**-fah
tax	el	im·**pues**·to	eem-**pwehss**-toh
total	el	to·**tal**	toh-**tahl**
transport	el	trans·**por**·te	trahnss-**pohr**-teh
VAT (value added tax)	el	I·VA	**ee**-vah

© 2000 Kathy Parsons, Spanish for Cruisers

What's included?

Is .... included?	¿Es**tá** in**clui**do ...	Ehss-**tah** een-**klwee**-doh...?
... the tax ...	... **el** im**pues**to?	... **ehl** eem-**pwehss**-toh?
... the transport ...	... **el** trans**por**te?	... **ehl** trahns-**pohr**-teh?

Guarantee

How long is the guarantee?	¿**Cuán**to **es el tiem**po **de** ga·ran**tí**a?	**Kwahn**-toh **ehss ehl tyehm**-poh **deh** gah-rahn-**tee**-ah?

Can you give me ...?

Can you give me ...	¿**Pue**·de **dar**·me	**Pweh**-deh **dahr**-meh...
... a discount?	... **un** des**cuen**to?	...**oon** dehs-**kwehn**-toh?
... an invoice, bill?	... **u**·na fac**tu**·ra?	...**oo**-nah fahk-**too**-rah?
... a copy?	... **u**·na **co**·pia?	...**oo**-nah **koh**-pyah?
... a bag?	... **u**·na **bol**·sa?	...**oo**-nah **bohl**-sah?
... a box?	... **u**·na **ca**·ja?	...**oo**-nah **kah**-hah?

© 2000 Kathy Parsons, Spanish for Cruisers

Returns and exchanges

Can I return this if it isn't the correct size?	¿**Pue**do re·gre**sar es**·to **si no es el** ta·**ma**·ño co·**rrec**·to?	**Pweh**-doh reh-greh-**sahr ehss**-toh **see noh ehss ehl** tah-**mah**-nyoh koh-**rrehk**-toh?
I want to exchange this for ...	**Quie**·ro cam·**biar es**·to **por** ...	**Kyeh**-roh kahm-**byahr ehss**-toh **pohr** ...
I need to return this ...	Ne·ce·**si**·to re·gre·**sar es**·to ...	Neh-seh-**see**-toh reh-greh-**sahr ehss**-toh..
... because it doesn't work.	... **por**·que **no** fun·**cio**·na.	... **pohr**-keh **noh** foon-**syoh**-nah.
... because it's no good, doesn't work, fit	... **por**·que **no sir**·ve	... **pohr**-keh **noh** seer-veh
... because it isn't the correct size.	... **por**·que **no es el** ta·**ma**·ño co·**rrec**·to.	... **pohr**-keh **noh ehss ehl** tah-**mah**-noyh koh-**rrehk**-toh.

I have.. ...	**Ten**·go ...	**Tehn**-goh ...
... the bill.	... **la** fac·**tu**·ra	... lah fahk-**too**-rah
... everything here..	... a·**quí to**·do.	... ah-**kee toh**-doh

By the way ...
When you pay for your purchase, the clerk may ask:

Do you have small change? *(a smaller denomination or correct change)*	¿**Tie**·ne sen·**ci**·llo?	**Tyeh**-neh sehn-**see**-yoh?

© 2000 Kathy Parsons, Spanish for Cruisers

hardware store	la	ferretería	feh-rreh-teh-**ree**-ah
marine hardware store	la	ferretería marina	feh-rreh-teh-**ree**-ah mah-**ree**-nah
store	la	**tien**da	**tyehn**-dah
parts	los	re**pues**tos	reh-**pwehss**-tohss
	las	**pie**zas	**pyeh**-sahss
	las	refac**cio**nes (Mexico)	reh-fahk-**syoh**-nehss
parts store	la	**tien**da **de** re**pues**tos	**tyehn**-dah **deh** reh-**pwehss**-tohss
automobile parts	los	re**pues**tos **de** auto**mó**viles	reh-**pwehss**-tohss **deh** ow-toh-**moh**-vee-lehss
plumbing parts	los	re**pues**tos **de** plome**rí**a	reh-**pwehss**-tohss **deh** ploh-meh-**ree**-ah
refrigeration parts	los	re**pues**tos **de** refrigera**ción**	reh-**pwehss**-tohss **deh** reh-free-heh-rah-**syohn**
repair or workshop	el	ta**ller**	tah-**yehr**
mechanic's shop	el	ta**ller** me**cá**ni**co**	tah-**yehr** meh-**kah**-nee-koh
welding shop	el	ta**ller de** solda**du**ra	tah-**yehr deh** sohl-dah-**doo**-rah
electric repair shop	el	ta**ller** e**léc**trico	tah-**yehr** eh-**lehk**-tree-koh
sail shop	el	ta**ller de ve**las	tah-**yehr deh veh**-lahss
boatyard	el	vara**de**ro	vah-rah-**deh**-roh
shipyard	el	asti**lle**ro	ahss-tee-**yeh**-roh
lumberyard	la	made**re**ra	mah-deh-**reh**-rah
factory	la	**fá**brica	**fah**-bree-kah

© 2000 Kathy Parsons, Spanish for Cruisers

mechanic	el	me·cá·ni·co	meh-**kah**-nee-koh
technician, repairman	el	**téc**·ni·co	**tehk**-nee-koh
diesel mechanic	el	me·**cá**·ni·co **die**·sel	meh-**kah**-nee-koh **dee**-sehl
outboard mechanic	el	me·**cá**·ni·co **de** fue·ra·**bor**·das	meh-**kah**-nee-koh **deh fweh**-rah-**bohr**-dahss
refrigeration repairman	el	**téc**·ni·co **de** re·fri·ge·ra·**ción**	**tehk**-nee-koh **deh** reh-free-heh-rah-**syohn**
welder	el	sol·da·**dor**	sohl-dah-**dohr**
electrician	el	e·lec·tri·**cis**·ta	eh-lehk-tree-**seess**-tah
carpenter	el	car·pin·**te**·ro	kahr-peen-**teh**-roh
upholsterer	el	ta·pi·**ce**·ro	tah-pee-**seh**-roh
manager	el	ge·**ren**·te	heh-**rehn**-teh

Asking about Places and Mechanics

I need a good ...	Ne·ce·si·to **un buen** ...	Neh-seh-**see**-toh **oon bwehn** ...
Where is the ...?	¿**Dón**·de es·**tá el** ...?	**Dohn**-deh ehss-**tah ehl** ... ?
Where is there a ...?	¿**Dón**·de **hay un** ...?	**Dohn**-deh **eye oon** ... ?
Is there a ... nearby?	¿**Hay un** ... **cer**·ca?	**Eye oon** ... **sehr**-kah?
Where can I buy ...?	¿**Dón**·de **pue**·do com·**prar** ...?	**Dohn**-deh **pweh**-doh kohm-**prahr** ... ?
Is there a ... that speaks English?	¿**Hay un** ... **que** ha·ble in·**glés**?	**Eye oon** ... **kay** ah-bleh een-**glehss**?
Can you send a ...?	¿**Pue**·de man·**dar un** ...?	**Pweh**-deh mahn-**dahr oon** ... ?

© 2000 Kathy Parsons, Spanish for Cruisers

Strategy for getting directions:

✓ Ask "Where is ...?"

✓ Glean as much as you can from the answer and hand gestures. Then, ...

✓ Ask a series of focused questions that will draw out short easier-to-understand answers, such as:

Is it near? ... Is it on this street? ... How many blocks?

This way? ... On the left? ... etc.

✓ Don't worry that you might be asking the same thing a person just tried to tell you.

✓ Follow the directions as far as you can, then stop and ask someone else for more directions.

Where is ...?		
Where is ...?	¿**Dón**·de es**tá** ...?	**Dohn**-deh ehss-**tah** ...?
Where is there ..?	¿**Dón**·de **hay** ...?	**Dohn**-deh **eye** ...?

Is it nearby?		
Is it near?	¿Es**tá cer**·ca?	Ehss-**tah sehr**-kah?
Is it far?	¿Es**tá le**·jos?	Ehss-**tah leh**-hohss?
Is it near ... *the market*?	¿ Es**tá cer**·ca **de** ...*el mercado*?	Ehss-**tah sehr**-kah **deh** ...*ehl mehr-kah-doh?*

© 2000 Kathy Parsons, Spanish for Cruisers

Is it on this street?

Is it on this street?	¿Está en esta calle?	Ehss-tah ehn ehss-tah kah-yeh?
What's the name of the street?	¿Cómo se llama la calle?	Koh-moh seh yah-mah lah kah-yeh?
This is the highway/road to ...?	¿Esta es la carretera a...?	Ehss-stah ehss lah kah-rreh-teh-rah ah ..?

Está (ehss-tah) means "it is", but esta (ehss-tah) means "this". Watch your accent!

How many blocks?

How many blocks?	¿Cuántas cuadras?	Kwahn-tahss kwah-drahss?
Is it on this block?	¿Está en esta cuadra?	Ehss-tah ehn ehss-tah kwah-drah?
Is it on the next block?	¿Está en la próxima cuadra?	Ehss-tah ehn lah pro-ksee-mah kwah-drah?
How many kilometers?	¿Cuántos kilómetros?	Kwahn-tohss kee-loh-meh-trohss?

On which side of the street?

On which side (of street)?	¿A qué lado?	Ah keh lah-doh?
On the left?	¿A la izquierda?	Ah lah ees-kyehr-dah?
On the right?	¿A la derecha?	Ah lah deh-reh-chah?

At the corner?

At the corner, intersection?	¿En la esquina?	Ehn lah ehss-kee-nah?
At the next corner?	¿En la próxima esquina?	Ehn lah proh-ksee-mah ehss-kee-nah?

© 2000 Kathy Parsons, Spanish for Cruisers

Turn left / right?

| Do I turn left? | ¿**Do**blo **a la** iz**quier**da? | **Doh**-bloh **ah lah** ees-**kyehr**-dah? |
| Do I turn right? | ¿**Do**blo **a la** de**re**cha? | **Doh**-bloh **ah lah** deh-**reh**-chah? |

This way?

| Is it this way? | ¿Es**tá por** a**quí**? | Ehss-**tah pohr** ah-**kee**? |
| Straight ahead? | ¿**To**do de**re**cho? | **Toh**-doh deh-**reh**-choh? |

Before, after, next to?

Before ...?	¿**An**tes **de** ...?	**Ahn**-tehss **deh** ... ?
After ...?	¿Des**pués de** ...?	Dehss-**pwehss deh** ... ?
Next to ...?	¿**Al la**do **de** ...?	**Ahl lah**-doh **deh** ... ?

street	la	**ca**lle	**kah**-yeh
road, highway	la	ca**rre**te**ra**	kah-rreh-**teh**-rah
corner	la	es**qui**na	ehss-**kee**-nah
block	la	**cua**dra	**kwah**-drah
side	el	**la**do	**lah**-doh

near, close	**cer**ca	**sehr**-kah
far	**le**jos	**leh**-hohss
this way	**por** a**quí**	**pohr** ah-**kee**
further on	**más** a**llá**	**más** ah-**yah**
(more there...!)		

© 2000 Kathy Parsons, Spanish for Cruisers

on the left, to the left	**a la** iz**quier**da	ah lah eess-**kyehr**-dah
on the right, to the right	**a la** de**re**cha	ah lah deh-**reh**-chah
straight ahead	**to**do de**re**cho	**toh**-doh deh-**reh**-choh
	de**re**cho	deh-**reh**-choh
	recto	**rehk**-toh
forward, ahead	a·de·**lan**·te	ah-deh-**lahn**-teh
backwards	a·**trás**	ah-**trahss**

a la derecha means "to the right" or
"on the right" but ...
derecho means "straight ahead"!

starboard	es·tri·**bor**	ehss-tree-**bohr**
port	ba·**bor**	bah-**bohr**

before ...	**an**·tes **de** ...	ahn-tehss **deh** ...
after ...	des·**pués de** ...	dehss-**pwehss** de ...
at the end of ...	**al** fi·**nal de** ...	ahl fee-**nahl deh** ...
across from ...	en·**fren**·te **de**	ehn-**frehn**-teh **deh** ...
next to ...	**al la**·do **de** ...	ahl **lah**-doh **deh** ...

It's not your fault that directions are so hard to understand...
Often, people will refer to landmarks you don't know. In Nicaragua when I used to ask for directions, people would answer "Turn left where that big tree used to be before the earthquake..."
That's why you need to take the lead and ask focused questions!

Again, please. *(repeat, please)*	**O**·tra **vez, por** fa·**vor.**	**Oh**-trah **vehss, pohr** fah-**vohr.**
Slower, please.	**Más** des·**pa**·cio, **por** fa·**vor.**	**Mahss** dehss-**pah**-syoh, **pohr** fah-**vohr.**

© 2000 Kathy Parsons, Spanish for Cruisers

Setting a time

At what time ...?	¿A qué ho·ra ... ?	Ah keh oh-rah ...?
When ...?	¿Cuán·do ...?	Kwahn-doh ...?
When are you/he/she coming?	¿Cuán·do vie·ne?	Kwahn-doh vyeh-neh?
When is he/she coming back?	¿Cuán·do vie·ne?	Kwahn-doh vyeh-neh?
Can you go out to my boat ...?	¿Pue·de ir a mi bar·co ...?	Pweh-deh eer ah mee bahr-koh ... ?
I need this by ...	Ne·ce·si·to es·to pa·ra ...	Neh-seh-see-toh ehss-toh pah-rah ...
I need to pick this up ...	Ne·ce·si·to re·co·ger es·to ...	Neh-seh-see-toh reh-koh-hehr ehss-toh ...
I have an appointment for/at ...	Ten·go u·na ci·ta pa·ra ...	Tehn-goh oo-nah see-tah pah-rah ...
I am going to leave ...	Voy a sa·lir ...	Voy ah sah-leer ...
I will come (back) ...	Ven·go ...	Vehn-goh ...
See you Monday. *	Nos ve·mos el lu·nes.	Nohss veh-mohss ehl loo-nehss.
See you tomorrow at 2. *	Nos ve·mos ma·ña·na a las dos.	Nohss veh-mohss mah-nyah-nah ah las dohss.

Good way to say goodbye. It confirms the agreement you made as to when you will meet or pick up your job.

now (soon...sort of)	a·ho·ra	ah-oh-rah	right now	a·ho·ra mis·mo	ah-oh-rah meess-moh
already, right now	ya	yah	in an hour	en u·na ho·ra	ehn oo-nah oh-rah
soon	pron·to	prohn-toh	as soon as possible	cuan·to an·tes	kwahn-toh ahn-tehss
late	tar·de	tahr-deh	in 30 minutes	en trein·ta mi·nu·tos	ehn trayn-tah mee-noo-tohss
later	más tar·de lue·go	mahss tahr-deh lweh-goh			
early	tem·pra·no	tehm-prah-noh			

© 2000 Kathy Parsons, Spanish for Cruisers

at ... o'clock

Time	Spanish	Pronunciation
1:00	**a la u**·na	ah lah oo-nah
2:00	**a las dos**	ah lahss dohss
3:00	**a las tres**	ah lahss trehss
4:00	**a las cua**·tro	ah lahss kwah-troh
5:00	**a las cin**·co	ah lahss seen-koh
6:00	**a las seis**	ah lahss sayss
7:00	**a las sie**·te	ah lahss syeh-teh
8:00	**a las o**·cho	ah lahss oh-choh
9:00	**a las nue**·ve	ah lahss nweh-veh
10:00	**a las diez**	ah lahss dyehss
11:00	**a las on**·ce	ah lahss ohn-seh
12:00	**a las do**·ce	ah lahss doh-seh

Time	Spanish	Pronunciation
12:30	**a las do**·ce y **trein**·ta *(at the 12 and 30)*	ah lahss doh-seh ee trayn-tah
half past 12	**a las do**·ce y me·dia *(at the 12 and half)*	ah lahss doh-seh ee meh-dyah

English	Spanish	Pronunciation
in the morning	**de la** ma·ña·na	deh lah mah-**nyah**-nah
in the afternoon	**de la tar**·de	deh lah **tahr**-deh
at night	**de la no**·che	deh lah **noh**-cheh

In English, you say "at 1 o'clock", "at 2 o'clock"
In Spanish you say "at the 1", "at the 2" (**la**, **las** mean *the*)
mañana means both *tomorrow* and *morning*

Days of the week

Day		Spanish	Pronunciation
Sunday	el	do·**min**·go	doh-**meen**-goh
Monday	el	**lu**·nes	loo-nehss
Tuesday	el	**mar**·tes	**mahr**-tehss
Wednesday	el	**miér**·co·les	**myehr**-koh-lehss
Thursday	el	**jue**·ves	**hweh**-vehss
Friday	el	**vier**·nes	**vyehr**-nehss
Saturday	el	**sá**·ba·do	**sah**-bah-doh

English	Spanish	Pronunciation
today	**hoy**	**oy**
tomorrow	ma·**ña**·na	mah-**nyah**-nah
yesterday	a·**yer**	ah-**yehr**
day after tomorrow	pa·**sa**·do ma·**ña**·na	pah-**sah**-doh mah-**nyah**-nah

English	Spanish	Pronunciation
next ... *Monday, Tuesday*	**el pró**·xi·mo *...lu·nes, mar·tes*	ehl proh-ksee-moh *...loo-nehss, mahr-tehss*

© 2000 Kathy Parsons, Spanish for Cruisers

These phrases will come in handy if you ever need to call for emergency help at sea. There are more phrases for describing your boat (pages 49-50), giving your location (pages 51-52), and talking on the radio (pages 53-54).

1. Call for help

May-Day May-Day	May-Day May-Day	(universal distress call in any language)
I need help.	Ne·ce·**si**·to a·**yu**·da.	Neh-seh-**see**-toh ah-**yoo**-dah.
I have an emergency.	**Ten**·go u·na e·mer·**gen**·cia.	**Tehn**-goh **oo**-nah eh-mehr-**hen**-syah.
It's an emergency.	**Es** u·na e·mer·**gen**·cia.	**Ehss oo**-nah eh-mehr-**hen**-syah.

2. Give your boat name

This is the sailboat ...	**Es**·te **es el** ve·**le**·ro ...	**Ehss**-teh **ehss ehl** veh-**leh**-roh ...
This is the yacht ...	**Es**·te **es el ya**·te ...	**Ehss**-teh **ehss ehl yah**-teh ...
The name of my boat is ...	**El nom**·bre **de mi bar**·co **es** ...	**Ehl nohm**-breh **deh mee bahr**-koh **ehss** ...

*The **Alphabet** is on page 15.*

3. Give your current location

My position is ...	**Mi** po·si·**ción es** ...	**Mee** poh-see-**syohn ehss** ...
... *xx* degrees	... *xx* **gra**·dos	... **grah**-dohss
... *xx.x* minutes North	*xx* **pun**·to *x* mi·**nu**·tos **nor**·te	... **poon**-toh ... mee-**noo**-tohss **nohr**-teh
... *xx.x* minutes West	*xx* **pun**·to *x* mi·**nu**·tos o·**es**·te	... **poon**-toh ... mee-**noo**-tohss oh-**ehss**-teh
... *xx.x* minutes South	*xx* **pun**·to *x* mi·**nu**·tos **sur**	... **poon**-toh ... mee-**noo**-tohss **soor**

*Substitute the appropriate numbers in place of xx. **Numbers** are on pages 29-31.*

4. Explain the problem

| My boat is sinking. | **Mi bar**·co **se** es·**tá** hun·**dien**·do. | **Mee bahr**-koh **seh** ehss-**tah** oon-**dyehn**-doh. |

© 2000 Kathy Parsons, Spanish for Cruisers

Fire aboard!	**Fue**go **a bor**do.	**Fweh**-goh ah **bohr**-doh.
Man overboard!	**Hom**bre **al a**gua!	**Ohm**-breh ahl **ah**-gwah!
I have had a collision.	**He** te**ni**do **un cho**que.	Eh teh-**nee**-doh **oon choh**-keh.
My boat is aground.	**Mi bar**co es**tá** en**ca**lla**do**.	Mee **bahr**-koh ehss-**tah** ehn-kah-**yah**-doh.
The engine won't run.	**El** mo**tor no** fun**cio**na.	Ehl moh-**tohr noh** foon-**syoh**-nah.
I cannot sail.	**No pue**do na**ve**gar.	Noh **pweh**-doh nah-veh-**gahr**.
The battery is dead.	**La** ba**te**ría es**tá muer**ta.	Lah bah-teh-**ree**-ah ehss-**tah mwehr**-tah.

5. Ask for help

I need ...	Ne**ce**si**to** ...	Neh-seh-**see**-toh ...
... help	... a**yu**da	... ah-**yoo**-dah
... diesel	... **die**sel	... **dee**-sehl
... gasoline	... ga**so**li**na** (_not_ **gas!**)	... gah-soh-**lee**-nah
... a tow to ...	... **un** re**mol**que **a** ...	... **oon** reh-**mohl**-keh ah ...
... a mechanic	... **un** me**cá**ni**co**	... **oon** meh-kah-nee-koh
... a diver	... un **bu**zo	... **oon** boo-soh
... a bilge pump	... u**na bom**ba **de** a**chi**que	... oo-nah **bohm**-bah **deh** ah-**chee**-keh
... help to enter the port	... a**yu**da **pa**ra en**trar al puer**to	... ah-**yoo**-dah **pah**-rah ehn-**trahr ahl pwehr**-toh
Can you bring ...?	¿**Pue**de tra**er** us**ted** ...?	**Pweh**-deh try-**ehr** ooss-**tehd** ...?
When are you coming?	¿**Cuán**do **vie**ne us**ted**?	**Kwahn**-doh **vyeh**-neh ooss-**tehd**?

© 2000 Kathy Parsons, Spanish for Cruisers

Give your name and nationality

My name is ...	Mi nombre es ...	Mee nohm-breh ehss ...
I am American.	Soy norteamericano.	Soy nohr-teh-ah-meh-ree-kah-noh.
We are American.	Somos norteamericanos.	Soh-mohss nohr-teh-ah-meh-ree-kah-nohss.
I am from Canada.	Soy de Canadá.	Soy deh Kah-nah-dah.
We are from Canada.	Somos de Canadá.	Soh-mohss deh Kah-nah-dah.
I am the captain.	Soy el capitán. *(male)*	Soy ehl kah-pee-tahn.
	Soy la capitán. *(female)*	Soy lah kah-pee-tahn.

Tell how many persons are aboard

There are ... people aboard.	Hay ... personas a bordo.	Eye ... pehr-soh-nahss ah bohr-doh.
There are ... crew.	Hay ... tripulantes.	Eye ... tree-poo-lahn-tehss.
There are no passengers.	No hay pasajeros.	Noh eye pah-sah-heh-rohss.

Give your length, draft and beam

The length is .... meters.	La eslora es .... metros.	Lah ehss-loh-rah ehss .... meh-trohss.
The draft is .... meters.	El calado es .... metros.	Ehl kah-lah-doh ehss ... meh-trohss.
The beam is .... meters.	La manga es .... metros.	Lah mahn-gah ehss ... meh-trohss.
The height is .... meters.	La altura es .... metros.	Lah ahl-too-rah ehss ... meh-trohss.

Numbers are on pages 29-31.
See page 158 for safety equipment.

© 2000 Kathy Parsons, Spanish for Cruisers

Describe the type of boat		
It is a sailboat.	**Es un** ve·le·ro.	Ehss oon veh-**leh**-roh.
It is a motor yacht.	**Es un** ya·te **de** mo·tor.	Ehss oon yah-teh **deh** moh-**tohr**.
It is a monohull.	**Es un** mo·no·**cas**·co.	Ehss oon moh-noh-**kahss**-koh.
It is a catamaran.	**Es un** ca·ta·ma·**rán**.	Ehss oon kah-tah-mah-**rahn**.

Tell the number of masts		
It has one mast.	**Tie**·ne **un más**·til.	**Tyeh**-neh oon **mahss**-teel.
It has two masts.	**Tie**·ne **dos más**·ti·les.	**Tyeh**-neh **dohss mahss**-tee-lehss.
It doesn't have a mast.	**No tie**·ne **más**·til.	Noh **tyeh**-neh **mahss**-teel.

Give the color of hull and sail covers		
The hull is ...	**El cas**·co **es** ...	Ehl **kahss**-koh **ehss** ...
The sail covers are ...	**Las fun**·das **de** ve·la **son** ...	Lahss **foon**-dahss **deh** veh-lah **sohn** ...
The awning is ..	**El tol**·do **es** ...	Ehl **tohl**-doh **ehss** ...

white	**blan**·co	**blahn**-koh
blue	a·**zul**	ah-**sool**
red	**ro**·jo	**roh**-hoh
green	**ver**·de	**vehr**-deh
black	**ne**·gro	**neh**-groh

gray	**gris** ·	**greess**
yellow	a·ma·**ri**·llo	ah-mah-**ree**-yoh
brown	ca·**fé**	kah-**feh**
orange	a·na·ran·**ja**·do	ah-nah-rahn-**hah**-doh
purple	mo·**ra**·do	moh-**rah**-doh

© 2000 Kathy Parsons, Spanish for Cruisers

Give your position.

My position is ...	Mi po·si·ción es ...	Mee poh-see-syohn ehss ...
I am at ...	Es·toy en ...	Ehss-toy ehn ...
... degrees	... gra·dos	... grah-dohss
... minutes	... mi·nu·tos	... mee-noo-tohss
... point (decimal point when giving latitude or longitude)	... pun·to	... poon-toh

Numbers are on pages 29-30

Give your latitude and longitude.

My latitude is ... North.	Mi la·ti·tud es ... nor·te.	Mee lah-tee-tood ehss ... nohr-teh.
My longitude is ... West.	Mi lon·gi·tud es ... o·es·te.	Mee lohn-hee-tood ehss ... oh-ehss-teh.
My latitude is ... South.	Mi la·ti·tud es ... sur.	Mee lah-tee-tood ehss ... soor.

Give your course and speed.

My course is ... degrees.	Mi rum·bo es ... gra·dos.	Mee room-boh ehss .. . grah-dohss.
My speed is ... knots.	Mi ve·lo·ci·dad es ... nu·dos.	Mee veh-loh-see-dahd ehss ... noo-dohss.
I am under sail.	Es·toy na·ve·gan·do a ve·la.	Ehss-toy nah-veh-gahn-doh ah veh-lah.
I am motoring.	Es·toy na·ve·gan·do a mo·tor.	Ehss-toy nah-veh-gahn-doh ah moh-tohr.
I am stopped.	Es·toy pa·ra·do.	Ehss-toy pah-rah-doh.
I am adrift.	Es·toy a la de·ri·va.	Ehss-toy ah la deh-ree-vah.
I am anchored.	Es·toy an·cla·do.	Ehss-toy ahn-klah-doh.
I am aground.	Es·toy en·ca·lla·do.	Ehss-toy ehn-kah-yah-doh.

© 2000 Kathy Parsons, Spanish for Cruisers

norte

noroeste   noreste

oeste este

suroeste   sureste

sur

I am ... miles from ... (place)	Estoy a ... millas de ...	Ehss-toy ah ... mee-yahss deh ...
I am ... miles ...	Estoy a ... millas ...	Ehss-toy ah ... mee-yahss ...
... to the North of ... (place)	... al norte de ...	... ahl nohr-teh deh ...
... to the East of ... (place)	... al este de ...	... ahl ehss-teh deh ...
... to the South of ... (place)	... al sur de ...	... ahl soor deh ...
... to the West of ... (place)	... al oeste de ...	... ahl oh-ehss-teh deh ...
... to the Northeast of ... (place)	... al noreste de ...	... ahl nohr-ehss-teh deh ...
... to the Southeast of ... (place)	... al sureste de ...	... ahl soor-ehss-teh deh ...
... to the Southwest of ... (place)	... al suroeste de ...	... ahl soor-oh-ehss-teh deh ...
...to the Northwest of ... (place)	... al noroeste de ...	... ahl nohr-oh-ehss-teh deh ...
Say when you will arrive.		
I am going to be at/in ... (place) ...	Voy a estar en ... (place) ...	Voy ah ehss-tahr ehn ...
... in 30 minutes.	... en treinta minutos.	... ehn trayn-tah mee-noo-tohss
... in 2 hours.	... en dos horas.	... ehn dohss oh-rahss
... at two in the afternoon.	... a las dos de la tarde.	... ah lahss dohss deh lah tahr-deh.

© 2000 Kathy Parsons, Spanish for Cruisers

"Velero, Velero, Velero ..."
(Sailboat, Sailboat, Sailboat...)

This is a common way that sailboats are hailed on the VHF radio – they may be calling you!

Radio Talk		
With whom am I speaking?	¿**Con quién ha**·blo?	**Kohn kyehn ah**-bloh?
I'm waiting on this channel.	Es·**pe**·ro **en es**·te ca·**nal**.	Ehss-**peh**-roh **ehn ehss**-teh kah-**nahl**.
I'm waiting on channel 16.	Es·**pe**·ro **en el** ca·**nal diez y seis**.	Ehss-**peh**-roh **ehn ehl** kah-**nahl dyehss ee sayss**.
I'm standing by.	Es·**toy a la** es·**cu**·cha.	Ehss-**toy ah lah** ehss-**koo**-chah.
Can you switch to 68?	¿**Pue**·de cam·**biar a seis o**·cho?	**Pweh**-deh kahm-**byahr ah sayss oh**-choh?
Over (on radio)	**Cam**·bio.	**Kahm**-byoh
Go ahead.	A·de·**lan**·te.	Ah-deh-**lahn**-teh.
Copied.	Co·**pia**·do.	Koh-**pyah**-doh.
Repeat, please.	Re·**pi**·ta, **por** fa·**vor**.	Reh-**pee**-tah, **pohr** fah-**vohr**.
Switch to another frequency.	**Cam**·bie **de** fre·**cuen**·cia.	**Kahm**-byeh **deh** freh-**kwehn**-syah.

© 2000 Kathy Parsons, Spanish for Cruisers

This frequency is busy.	**Es**ta fre·**cuen**·cia es·**tá** o·cu·**pa**da.	**Ehss**-tah freh-**kwehn**-syah ehss-**tah** oh-koo-**pah**-dah.
This frequency is busy with an emergency.	**Es**ta fre·**cuen**·cia es·**tá** o·cu·pa·da **con** u·na e·mer·**gen**·cia.	**Ehss**-tah freh-**kwehn**-syah ehss-**tah** oh-koo-**pah**-dah **kohn** oo-nah eh-mehr-**heh**-syah.
My call sign is ...	**Mi** in·di·**ca**·ti·vo **de** lla·**ma**da **es** ...	**Mee** een-dee-kah-**tee**-voh **deh** yah-**mah**-dah **ehss** ...

Again, please. *(repeat, please)*	**O**·tra **vez, por** fa·**vor**.	**Oh**-trah **vehss, pohr** fah-**vohr**.
Slower, please.	**Más** des·**pa**·cio, **por** fa·**vor**.	**Mahss** dehss-**pah**-syoh, **pohr** fah-**vohr**.

See pages 153-154 for more radio terms.

Spell out your boat name in Spanish:

Use this area to spell out your boat name in the Spanish alphabet in case you are ever asked to give your boat name on the radio. (The Alphabet is on page 15.) Example: Name: R   O   M   A   N   C   E

Pronunciation: **eh**-reh **oh** **eh**-meh **ah** **eh**-neh **seh** **eh**

Your boat name:

Pronunciation:

© 2000 Kathy Parsons, Spanish for Cruisers

8.   **Emergencies:**   **Talking on the Radio**   54

Here are the units you'll need to give your boat's measurements or describe the dimensions of hardware, canvas, or carpentry items that you need. Pages 59 and 60 show you how to build sentences to ask for parts of a certain size.

1 meter = 3.281 feet

Measurements	las	Medidas	meh-**dee**-dahss
length	el	**lar**go	**lahr**-goh
	la	longi**tud**	lohn-hee-**tood**
height	el	**al**to	**ahl**-toh
	la	al**tu**ra	ahl-**too**-rah
width	el	**an**cho	**ahn**-choh
depth	la	profundi**dad**	proh-foon-dee-**dahd**
	el	**hon**do	**ohn**-doh
diameter	el	di**á**metro	dee-ah-meh-troh
internal diameter	el	di**á**metro in**ter**no	dee-ah-meh-troh een-**tehr**-noh
external diameter	el	di**á**metro ex**ter**no	dee-ah-meh-troh ehkss-**tehr**-noh
thickness	el	**grue**so	**grweh**-soh
size	el	ta**ma**ño	tah-**mah**-nyoh

meters	feet
1	3.3
2	6.6
3	9.8
4	13.1
5	16.4
6	19.7
7	23.0
8	26.2
9	29.5
10	32.8
11	36.1
12	39.4
12	39.4
13	42.7
14	45.9
15	49.2
16	52.5
17	55.8
18	59.1

Boat Measurements			
length-over-all	la	es**lo**ra	ehss-**loh**-rah
beam	la	**man**ga	**mahn**-gah
draft	el	ca**la**do	kah-**lah**-doh
	el	pun**tal**	poon-**tahl**

© 2000 Kathy Parsons, Spanish for Cruisers

Units			
meters	los	**me**tros	**meh**-trohss
millimeters	los	mi**lí**metros	mee-**lee**-meh-trohss
centimeters	los	cen**tí**metros	sehn-**tee**-meh-trohss
inches	las	pul**ga**das	pool-**gah**-dahss
feet	los	**pies**	**pyehss**
square feet	los	**pies** cua**dra**dos	**pyehss** kwah-**drah**-dohss
kilometers	los	ki**ló**metros	kee-**loh**-meh-trohss
meters	los	**me**tros	**meh**-trohss
miles	las	**mi**llas	**mee**-yahss
nautical miles	las	**mi**llas ma**ri**nas	**mee**-yahss mah-**ree**-nahss
knots	los	**nu**dos	**noo**-dohss

Record your boat's measurements in meters here:

La es**lo**ra **es** _____ **me**tros.
(length)
La manga **es** _____ **me**tros.
(beam)
El ca**la**do **es** _____ **me**tros.
(draft)

1	foot	=	0.305	meter
1	meter	=	3.281	feet
1	yard	=	0.914	meter
1	meter	=	1.094	yards
1	square yard	=	0.836	square meters

1	statute mile	=	1.61	kilometers
1	nautical mile	=	1.85	kilometers
1	kilometer	=	0.621	statute mile
1	kilometer	=	0.540	nautical mile

1	millimeter	=	0.039	inch
1	centimeter	=	0.394	inch
1	inch	=	2.54	centimeters

© 2000 Kathy Parsons, Spanish for Cruisers

9. **Measurements:** Length and Distance 56

Volume	el	volumen	voh-loo-mehn
liters	los	litros	lee-trohss
milliliters	los	mililitros	mee-lee-lee-trohss
gallons	los	galones	gah-loh-nehss

Weight	el	peso	peh-soh
kilos	los	kilos	kee-lohss
pounds	las	libras	lee-brahss
ounces	las	onzas	ohn-sahss
tons	las	toneladas	toh-neh-lah-dahss

Temperature	la	temperatura	tehm-peh-rah-too-rah
degrees	los	grados	grah-dohss
degrees Cent.	los	grados centígrados	grah-dohss sehn-tee-grah-dohss

Electrical			
voltage	el	voltaje	vohl-tah-heh
volts	los	voltios	vohl-tyohss
amps	los	amperios	ahm-peh-ryohss
watts	los	watts	wahts

© 2000 Kathy Parsons, Spanish for Cruisers

Engine related			
horsepower	los	ca·**ba**·llos	kah-**bah**-yohss
revolutions	las	re·vo·lu·**cio**·nes	reh-voh-loo-**syoh**-nehss
RPM		RPM	**Eh**-reh **Peh Eh**-meh
pressure	la	pre·**sión**	preh-**syohn**
PSI		PSI	**Peh Eh**-seh **Ee**

1	liter	=	1.057	quarts (US)
1	liter	=	0.264	gallon (US)
1	liter	=	34	ounces
1	gallon (US)	=	3.785	liters
1	quart (US)	=	0.946	liter
1	ounce (fluid)	=	29.6	milliliters

1	kilogram	=	2.2	pounds
1	pound	=	0.454	kilogram

(degrees Fahrenheit – 32) x 5/9 = degrees Celsius/Centigrade
(degrees Celsius x 9/5) + 32   = degrees Fahrenheit

© 2000 Kathy Parsons, Spanish for Cruisers

	In Spanish, you say:	2 inches **of length**	(dos pulgadas **de largo**)
	not:	2 inches long	
	In Spanish, you say:	2 inches **of width**	(dos pulgadas **de ancho**)
	not:	2 inches wide	
	In Spanish, you say:	2 inches **of thickness**	(dos pulgadas **de grueso**)
	not:	2 inches thick	

Same applies to **height**, **depth**...

**I need** ... (something) ... of ... (so many inches) ... **of length.**		
I need...	Ne·ce·si·to ...	Neh-seh-**see**-toh ...
... a bolt (screw) ...	... **un** tor·**ni**·llo...	... **oon** tohr-**nee**-yoh ...
... (of) 2 inches ...	... **de dos** pul·ga·das ...	... **deh dos** pool-**gah**-dahss ...
... of length.	.. **de lar**·go.	... **deh lahr**-goh.

**I need** ... (something) ... of ... (so many inches) ... **of width.**		
I need...	Ne·ce·si·to ...	Neh-seh-**see**-toh ...
... 4 bolts (screws) ...	... **4** tor·**ni**·llos...	... **kwah**-troh tohr-**nee**-yohss ...
... (of) ½ inch ...	... **de me**·dia pul·ga·da ...	... **deh meh**-dyah pool-**gah**-dah ...
... of width.	.. **de an**·cho.	... **deh ahn**-choh.

© 2000 Kathy Parsons, Spanish for Cruisers

I need ... (something) ... of ... (so many millimeters) ... of internal diameter.		
I need...	Ne·ce·si·to ...	Neh-seh-**see**-toh ...
... a pipe ...	... **un tu**·bo...	... **oon too**-boh ...
... (of) 20 millimeters ...	... **de** 20 mi·lí·me·tros...	... **deh vayn**-teh mee-lee-meh-trohss ...
...of internal diameter.	.. **de** di·**á**·me·tro in·ter·no.	... **deh** dee-ah-meh-troh een-**tehr**-noh.

I need ... (something) ... of ... (so many inches) ... of external diameter.		
I need...	Ne·ce·si·to ...	Neh-seh-**see**-toh ...
... a hose ...	... **u**·na man·**gue**·ra ...	... oo-nah mahn-**gheh**-rah ...
... (of) ½ inch ...	... **de me**·dia pul·ga·da ...	... **deh meh**-dyah pool-**gah**-dah ...
...of external diameter.	.. **de** di·**á**·me·tro ex·**ter**·no.	... **deh** dee-ah-meh-troh ehkss-**tehr**-noh.

I need ... (something) ... of ... (so many inches) ... of thickness.		
I need...	Ne·ce·si·to ...	Neh-seh-**see**-toh ...
... a washer ...	... **u**·na a·ran·**de**·la ... (ron·**da**·na -*Mexico*)	... oo-nah ah-rahn-**deh**-lah ...
... (of) ¾ of an inch...	... **de tres cuar**·tos **de** pul·ga·das ...	... **deh trehss kwahr**-tohss **deh** pool-**gah**-dahss ...
... of thickness.	.. **de grue**·so.	... **deh grweh**-soh.

© 2000 Kathy Parsons, Spanish for Cruisers

metal	el	me·tal	meh-tahl
alloy	la	a·le·a·**ción**	ah-leh-ah-**syohn**
aluminum	el	a·lu·**mi**·nio	ah-loo-**mee**-nyoh
brass	el	la·**tón**	lah-**tohn**
bronze	el	**bron**·ce	**brohn**-seh
cast iron	el	**hie**·rro fun·**di**·do	**yeh**-roh foon-**dee**-doh
chrome	el	**cro**·mo	**kroh**-moh
copper	el	**co**·bre	**koh**-breh
galvanized steel	el	a·**ce**·ro gal·va·ni·**za**·do	ah-**seh**-roh gahl-vah-nee-**sah**-doh
gold	el	**o**·ro	**oh**-roh
hardened steel	el	me·**tal du**·ro	meh-**tahl doo**-roh
iron	el	**hie**·rro	**yeh**-roh
	el	**fie**·rro	**fyeh**-roh
lead	el	**plo**·mo	**ploh**-moh
nickel	el	**ní**·quel	**nee**-kehl
silicon bronze	el	**bron**·ce si·**li**·cio	**brohn**-seh see-lee-**syoh**
silver	la	**pla**·ta	**plah**-tah
stainless steel	el	a·**ce**·ro in·o·xi·**da**·ble	ah-**seh**-roh een-ohk-see-**dah**-bleh
steel	el	a·**ce**·ro	ah-**seh**-roh
tin	el	es·**ta**·ño	ehss-**tah**-nyoh
zinc	el	**zinc**	**seenk**

© 2000 Kathy Parsons, Spanish for Cruisers

wood	la	ma·de·ra	mah-**deh**-rah
ash	el	**fres**·no	**frehss**-noh
balsawood	la	ma·de·ra **de bal**·sa	mah-**deh**-rah **deh bahl**-sah
board	la	**ta**·bla	**tah**-blah
cedar	el	**ce**·dro	**seh**-droh
dry wood	la	ma·de·ra **se**·ca	mah-**deh**-rah **seh**-kah
grain	la	**fi**·bra	**fee**-brah
green (unseasoned) wood	la	ma·de·ra **ver**·de	mah-**deh**-rah **vehr**-deh
laminated		la·mi·**na**·do	lah-mee-**nah**-doh
lignum vitae	el	**pa**·lo **san**·to	**pah**-loh **sahn**-toh
mahogany	la	ca·**o**·ba	kah-**oh**-bah
oak	el	**ro**·ble	**roh**-bleh
particle board	la	ma·de·ra com·pri·**mi**·da	mah-**deh**-rah kohm-pree-**mee**-dah
pine	el	**pi**·no	**pee**-noh
plywood	el	con·tra·cha·**pa**·do	kohn-trah-chah-**pah**-doh
	el	tri·**play** *(Mexico)*	tree-**pleye**
seasoned wood	la	ma·de·ra cu·**ra**·da	mah-**deh**-rah koo-**rah**-dah
spruce	el	a·**be**·to	ah-**beh**-toh
teak	la	**te**·ca	**teh**-kah
veneer	la	**cha**·pa **de** ma·**de**·ra	**chah**-pah **deh** mah-**deh**-rah

© 2000 Kathy Parsons, Spanish for Cruisers

acrylic	el	a·**crí**·li·co	ah-**kree**-lee-koh
asbestos	el	as·**bes**·to	ahss-**behss**-toh
canvas	la	**lo**·na	loh-nah
carbon	el	car·**bón**	kahr-**bohn**
carbon fiber	la	**fi**·bra **de** car·**bo**·no	**fee**-brah **deh** kahr-**boh**-noh
cork	el	**cor**·cho	**kohr**-choh
cotton	el	al·go·**dón**	ahl-goh-**dohn**
enamel	el	es·**mal**·te	ehss-**mahl**-teh
fabric	la	**te**·la *(not material or fábrica, fábrica means factory)*	teh-lah
fiberglass	la	**fi**·bra **de** vi·drio	**fee**-brah **deh** **vee**-dryoh
foam rubber	la	**go**·ma es·**pu**·ma	**goh**-mah ehss-**poo**-mah
	el	**hu**·le es·**pu**·ma	**oo**-leh ehss-**poo**-mah
foam rubber (open-cell)	la	**go**·ma es·**pu**·ma **sua**·ve	**goh**-mah ehss-**poo**-mah **swah**-veh
	el	**hu**·le es·**pu**·ma **ba**·ja den·si·**dad**	**oo**-leh ehss-**poo**-mah **bah**-hah dehn-see-**dahd**
foam rubber (closed-cell)	la	**go**·ma es·**pu**·ma **du**·ra	**goh**-mah ehss-**poo**-mah **doo**-rah
	la	**go**·ma es·**pu**·ma com·pri·**mi**·da	**goh**-mah ehss-**poo**-mah kohm-pree-**mee**-dah
	el	**hu**·le es·**pu**·ma **al**·ta den·si·**dad**	**oo**-leh ehss-**poo**-mah **ahl**-tah dehn-see-**dahd**

© 2000 Kathy Parsons, Spanish for Cruisers

glass	el	**vi**·drio	**vee**-dryoh
Kevlar	el	**Kév**·lar	**Kehv**-lahr
leather	el	**cue**·ro	**kweh**-roh
	la	**piel**	**pyehl**
Neoprene	el	ne·o·**pre**·no	neh-oh-**preh**-noh
nylon	el	**ny**·lon / **nai**·lon	**neye**-lohn
paper	el	pa·**pel**	pah-**pehl**
plastic	el	**plás**·ti·co	**plahss**-tee-koh
PVC	el	**PVC**	peh-veh-**seh**
resin	la	re·**si**·na	reh-**see**-nah
rubber	la	**go**·ma	**goh**-mah
	el	**hu**·le	**oo**-leh
Teflon	el	te·**flón**	teh-**flohn**
wool	la	**la**·na	**lah**-nah

What's it (made) of?	¿**De qué es**?	**Deh keh ehss**?

© 2000 Kathy Parsons, Spanish for Cruisers

screw, bolt	el	tor·**ni**·llo	tohr-**nee**-yoh
	el	**per**·no *(occasionally)*	**pehr**-noh
machine screw	el	tor·**ni**·llo **pa**·ra me·**ta**·les	tohr-**nee**-yoh **pah**-rah meh-**tah**-lehss
	el	tor·**ni**·llo **má**·qui·na	tohr-**nee**-yoh **mah**-kee-nah
wood screw	el	tor·**ni**·llo **pa**·ra ma·**de**·ra	tohr-**nee**-yoh **pah**-rah mah-**deh**-rah
set or grub screw	el	tor·**ni**·llo **sin** ca·**be**·za	tohr-**nee**-yoh **seen** kah-**beh**-sah
	el	pri·sio·**ne**·ro	pree-syoh-**neh**-roh
stud	el	**bir**·lo	**beer**-loh
threaded rod	el	es·**pá**·rra·go	ehss-**pah**-rrah-goh
	head (of bolt)	la	ca·**be**·za	kah-**beh**-sah
⊖	screw (slotted)	el	tor·**ni**·llo **pla**·no	tohr-**nee**-yoh **plah**-noh
⊗	screw (Phillips)	el	tor·**ni**·llo **de** es·**trí**·a *(Caribbean)*	tohr-**nee**-yoh **deh** ehss-**tree**-ah
		el	tor·**ni**·llo **en cruz** *(Mexico)*	tohr-**nee**-yoh **ehn kroos**
		el	tor·**ni**·llo "**Phil**·lips"	tohr-**nee**-yoh **fee**-leeps
⊖	slot	la	ra·**nu**·ra	rah-**nooh**-rah
⬣	hex head		... **de** ca·**be**·za he·xa·go·**nal**	**deh** kah-**beh**-sah ehk-sah-goh-**nahl**
■	square head		... **de** ca·**be**·za cua·**dra**·da	**deh** kah-**beh**-sah kwah-**drah**-dah
◉	allen head		... **de** ca·**be**·za **a**·llen	**deh** kah-**beh**-sah **ah**-lehn
Y	flat head		... **de** ca·**be**·za **pla**·na	**deh** kah-**beh**-sah **plah**-nah

© 2000 Kathy Parsons, Spanish for Cruisers

round head		... de cabeza redonda	**deh** kah-**beh**-sah reh-**dohn**-dah
oval head		... de cabeza ovalada	**deh** kah-**beh**-sah oh-vah-**lah**-dah
countersunk		... de cabeza avellanada	**deh** kah-**beh**-sah ah-veh-yah-**nah**-dah
threads *(of screw)*	las	**ros**cas	**rohss**-kahss
fine thread		... **de ros**ca **fi**na	**deh rohss**-kah **fee**-nah
coarse thread		... **de ros**ca **grue**sa	**deh rohss**-kah **grweh**-sah
standard thread		... **de ros**ca **stan**dard	**deh rohss**-kah ess-**tahn**-dard
millimeter thread		... **de ros**ca milli**mé**trica	**deh rohss**-kah mee-lee-**meh**-tree-kah
self-tapping		... autorros**can**te	ow-toh-rrohss-**kahn**-teh
18 threads per inch		18 **ros**cas **la** pul**ga**da	18 **rohss**-kahss **lah** pool-**gah**-dah
metric		... **mé**trico	**meh**-tree-koh
standard		... **stan**dard	ess-**tahn**-dard
metric *(size)* 4		**mé**trico **cua**tro	**meh**-tree-koh **kwah**-troh
2 inches long *(of 2" of length)*		**de dos** pul**ga**das **de lar**go	**deh dohss** pool-**gah**-dahss **deh lahr**-goh
hole	el	agu**je**ro	ah-goo-**heh**-roh
with a collar		... **con un** co**llar**	**kohn oon** koh-**yahr**
with a hole		... **con un** agu**je**ro	**kohn oon** ah-goo-**heh**-roh
...of stainless steel		... **de** a**ce**ro inoxi**da**ble	**deh** ah-**seh**-roh een-oh-ksee-**dah**-bleh
...of galvanized steel		... **de** a**ce**ro galvani**za**do	**deh** ah-**seh**-roh gahl-vah-nee-**sah**-doh

© 2000 Kathy Parsons, Spanish for Cruisers

11. **Hardware:** Bolts and Screws **66**

nut	la	**tuer**ca	**twehr**-kah
locknut	la	con·tra·**tuer**·ca	kohn-trah-**twehr**-kah
	la	**tuer**·ca **de** se·gu·ri·**dad**	**twehr**-kah **deh** seh-goo-ree-**dahd**
wingnut	la	**tuer**·ca ma·ri·**po**·sa	**twehr**-kah mah-ree-**poh**-sah
castellated nut	la	**tuer**·ca en·cas·ti·**lla**·da	**twehr**-kah ehn-kahss-tee-**yah**-dah
cap nut	la	**tuer**·ca **de ta**·pa	**twehr**-kah **deh tah**-pah
cone nut	la	**tuer**·ca **có**·ni·ca	**twehr**-kah **koh**-nee-kah
washer	la	a·ran·**de**·la	ah-rahn-**deh**-lah
	la	ron·**da**·na *(Mexico)*	rohn-**dah**-nah
flat washer	la	a·ran·**de**·la **pla**·na	ah-rahn-**deh**-lah **plah**-nah
	la	ron·**da**·na **pla**·na *(Mexico)*	rohn-**dah**-nah **plah**-nah
lock or spring washer	la	a·ran·**de**·la a·**bier**·ta	ah-rahn-**deh**-lah ah-**byehr**-tah
	la	a·ran·**de**·la **de** pre·**sión**	ah-rahn-**deh**-lah **deh** preh-**syohn**
	la	ron·**da**·na **de** pre·**sión** *(Mexico)*	rohn-**dah**-nah **deh** preh-**syohn**
star washer	la	a·ran·**de**·la **de** es·**tre**·lla	ah-rahn-**deh**-lah **deh** ehss-**treh**-yah
	la	ron·**da**·na **de** es·**tre**·lla *(Mexico)*	rohn-**dah**-nah **deh** ehss-**treh**-yah
plate washer	la	a·ran·**de**·la **de pla**·ca	ah-rahn-**deh**-lah **deh plah**-kah
	la	ron·**da**·na **de pla**·ca *(Mexico)*	rohn-**dah**-nah **deh plah**-kah

© 2000 Kathy Parsons, Spanish for Cruisers

| spacer | el | se·pa·ra·**dor** | seh-pah-rah-**dohr** |
| | el | es·pa·cia·**dor** | ehss-pah-syah-**dohr** |

pin	el	pa·sa·**dor**	pah-sah-**dohr**
cotter pin	la	cha·**ve**·ta	chah-**veh**-tah
	el	pa·sa·**dor** a·**bier**·to	pah-sah-**dohr** ah-**byehr**-toh
	la	cu·**pi**·lla *(Venezuela)*	koo-**pee**-yah
split pin	el	pa·sa·**dor** a·**bier**·to	pah-sah-**dohr** ah-**byehr**-toh
key	la	**lla**·ve	**yah**-veh
ring	el	a·**ni**·llo	ah-**nee**-yoh
circlip, retaining ring	el	"cir-**clip**"	seer-**kleep**
	el	se·**gu**·ro	seh-**goo**-roh
	el	a·**ni**·llo **de** re·ten·**ción**	ah-**nee**-yoh **deh** reh-tehn-**syohn**

... of stainless steel	... **de** a·**ce**·ro in·ox·i·**da**·ble	ah-**seh**-roh een-oh-ksee-**dah**-bleh
... of galvanized steel	... **de** a·**ce**·ro gal·va·ni·**za**·do	ah-**seh**-roh gahl-vah-nee-**sah**-doh
... of bronze	... **de bron**·ce	**deh brohn**-seh
... of aluminum	... **de** a·lu·**mi**·nio	**deh** ah-loo-**mee**-nyoh

© 2000 Kathy Parsons, Spanish for Cruisers

11.   Hardware: Nuts, Washers, Other Fasteners   **68**

gasket	la	**jun**ta	**hoon**-tah
	el	em**pa**que *(Mexico)*	ehm-**pah**-keh
	la	em·pa·ca·**du**·ra *(Venezuela)*	ehm-pah-kah-**doo**-rah
(of) cork		... **de cor**·cho	**kohr**-choh
(of) rubber		... **de go**·ma	**deh goh**-mah
		... **de hu**·le	**deh** oo-leh
(of) asbestos		... **de** as·**bes**·to	**deh** ahss-**behss**-toh
O-ring	el	**O**-ring	**oh**-reeng
	el	a·**ni**·llo **en O**	ah-**nee**-yoh **ehn oh**
seal	el	re·**tén**	reh-**tehn**
	el	**se**·llo	**seh**-yoh
	el	re·te·ne·**dor**	reh-teh-neh-**dohr**
	la	es·to·**pe**·ra *(Venezuela)*	ehss-toh-**peh**-rah
retainer	el	re·**tén**	reh-**tehn**
	el	re·te·ne·**dor**	reh-teh-neh-**dohr**
packing	la	em·pa·que·ta·**du**·ra	ehm-pah-keh-tah-**doo**-rah
gasket cement	el	ce·**men**·to **pa**·ra **jun**·ta	seh-**mehn**-toh **pah**-rah **hoon**-tah
high-temperature gasket cement	el	ce·**men**·to **pa**·ra **jun**·ta **de al**·ta tem·pe·ra·**tu**·ra	seh-**mehn**-toh pah-rah **hoon**-tah **deh ahl**-tah tehm-peh-rah-**too**-rah

© 2000 Kathy Parsons, Spanish for Cruisers

bearing	el	co·ji·**ne**·te	koh-hee-**neh**-teh
	el	ba·**le**·ro *(Mexico)*	bah-**leh**-roh
	la	**ca**·ja **de bo**·las	**kah-hah deh boh**-lahss
	el	ro·da·**mien**·to	roh-dah-**myehn**-toh
ball bearing	el	co·ji·**ne**·te **de bo**·las	koh-hee-**neh**-te **deh boh**-lahss
	la	**ca**·ja **de bo**·las	**kah-hah deh boh**-lahss
	el	ba·**le**·ro *(Mexico)*	bah-**leh**-roh
needle bearing	el	co·ji·**ne**·te **de** a·**gu**·jas	koh-hee-**neh**-teh **deh** ah-**goo**-hahss
	el	ba·**le**·ro **de** a·**gu**·jas *(Mexico)*	bah-**leh**-roh **deh** ah-**goo**-hahss
roller bearing	el	co·ji·**ne**·te **de** ro·**di**·llos	koh-hee-**neh**-teh **deh** roh-**dee**-yohss
	el	ba·**le**·ro **de** ro·**di**·llos	bah-**leh**-roh **deh** roh-**dee**-yohss
	la	ro·li·**ne**·ra *(Venezuela)*	roh-lee-**neh**-rah
tapered roller bearing	el	co·ji·**ne**·te **de** ro·**di**·llos a·hu·**sa**·dos	koh-hee-**neh**-teh **deh** roh-**dee**-yohss ah-oo-**sah**-dohss
bearing cage	la	**jau**·la **de** co·ji·**ne**·te	**how**-lah **deh** koh-hee-**neh**-teh
	el	por·ta·ro·da·**mien**·to	pohr-tah-roh-dah-**myehn**-toh
bearing cup	la	**ta**·za **de** co·ji·**ne**·te	**tah**-sah **deh** koh-hee-**neh**-teh
bearing race	la	**pis**·ta **de** co·ji·**ne**·te	**peess**-tah **deh** koh-hee-**neh**-teh
thrust bearing	el	co·ji·**ne**·te **de** em·**pu**·je	koh-hee-**neh**-teh **deh** ehm-**poo**-heh
bushing	el	**bu**·je	**boo**-heh
	el	cas·**qui**·llo	kahss-**kee**-yoh
split bushing	el	**bu**·je par·**ti**·do	**boo**-heh pahr-**tee**-doh

© 2000 Kathy Parsons, Spanish for Cruisers

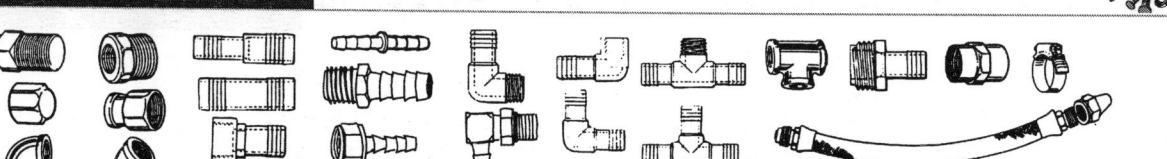

hose	la	man·**gue**·ra	mahn-**gheh**-rah
high-pressure hose	la	man·**gue**·ra **de al**·ta pre·**sión**	mahn-**gheh**-rah **deh ahl**-tah preh-**syohn**
wire-reinforced hose	la	man·**gue**·ra re·for·za·da **con** a·**lam**·bre	mahn-**gheh**-rah reh-fohr-**sah**-dah **kohn** ah-**lahm**-breh
hydraulic hose	la	man·**gue**·ra hi·**dráu**·li·ca	mahn-**gheh**-rah ee-**drow**-lee-kah
fuel hose	la	man·**gue**·ra **pa**·ra com·bus·**ti**·ble	mahn-**gheh**-rah **pah**-rah kohm-booss-**tee**-bleh
pipe	el	**tu**·bo	**too**-boh
tubing	la	tu·be·**rí**·a	too-beh-**ree**-ah
thick-walled		... **de** pa·**red grue**·sa	... **deh** pah-**rehd grweh**-sah
thin-walled		... **de** pa·**red** del·ga·da	... **deh** pah-**rehd** dehl-**gah**-dah
double-walled		... **de** pa·**red do**·ble	... **deh** pah-**rehd doh**-bleh
connector	la	co·ne·**xión**	koh-neh-**ksyohn**
pipe connector	la	co·ne·**xión pa**·ra **tu**·bos	koh-neh-**ksyohn pah**-rah **too**-bohss
hose connection	la	co·ne·**xión pa**·ra man·**gue**·ras	koh-neh-**ksyohn pah**-rah mahn-**gheh**-rahss
exterior thread	la	**ros**·ca ex·te·**rior**	**rohss**-kah ehkss-teh-**ryohr**
interior thread	la	**ros**·ca in·te·**rior**	**rohss**-kah een-teh-**ryohr**

© 2000 Kathy Parsons, Spanish for Cruisers

male *(threads, etc.)*		**ma**·cho	**mah**-choh
female *(threads, etc.)*		**hem**·bra	**ehm**-brah
nipple (close/short)	el	**ni**·ple (**cor**·to)	**nee**-pleh (**kohr**-toh)
threaded nipple	el	**ni**·ple **de ros**·ca	**nee**-pleh **deh rohss**-kah
T-connector	el	**ni**·ple **en for**·ma **T**	**nee**-pleh **ehn fohr**-mah **teh**
reducer	la	re·duc·**ción**	reh-dook-**syohn**
flare fitting	el	ac·ce·**so**·rio a·bo·car·**da**·do	ahk-seh-**soh**-ryoh ah-boh-kahr-**dah**-doh
compression fitting	el	ac·ce·**so**·rio **de** com·pre·**sión**	ahk-seh-**soh**-ryoh **deh** kohm-preh-**syohn**
elbow	el	**co**·do	**koh**-doh
elbow (90°)	el	**co**·do **de** 90 **gra**·dos	**koh**-doh **de** noh-**vehn**-tah **grah**-dohss
clamp, hose clamp	la	a·bra·za·**de**·ra	ah-brah-sah-**deh**-rah
plug	el	ta·**pón**	tah-**pohn**
valve	la	**vál**·vu·la	**vahl**-voo-lah
	la	**lla**·ve	**yah**-veh
check or 1-way valve	la	**vál**·vu·la "**check**"	**vahl**-voo-lah **chehk**
	la	**vál**·vu·la **de an**·ti-re·**tor**·no	**vahl**-voo-lah **deh** ahn-tee-reh-**tohr**-noh
3-way valve	la	**vál**·vu·la **de** des·**ví**·o	**vahl**-voo-lah **deh** dehss-**vee**-oh
shut-off valve	la	**vál**·vu·la **de cie**·rre	**vahl**-voo-lah **deh syeh**-rreh
ball valve	la	**vál**·vu·la **de bo**·la	**vahl**-voo-lah **deh boh**-lah
gate valve	la	**vál**·vu·la **de** com·**puer**·ta	**vahl**-voo-lah **deh** kohm-**pwehr**-tah

© 2000 Kathy Parsons, Spanish for Cruisers

bar	la	**ba**·rra	**bah**-rrah
rod	la	va·**ri**·lla	vah-**ree**-yah
threaded rod	la	va·**ri**·lla ros·**ca**·da	vah-**ree**-yah rohss-**kah**-dah
cable	el	**ca**·ble	**kah**-bleh
dowel	la	es·**pi**·ga	ehss-**pee**-gah
mount, bracket	el	so·**por**·te	soh-**pohr**-teh
plate	la	**pla**·ca	**plah**-kah
	la	**plan**·cha	**plahn**-chah
sheet metal	la	**lá**·mi·na *(thinner)*	**lah**-mee-nah
	la	**cha**·pa *(thicker)*	**chah**-pah
shim	el	**cal**·zo	**kahl**-soh
spring	el	re·**sor**·te	reh-**sohr**-teh
	el	**spring**	ehss-**preeng**

Nails, rivets, staples

nail	el	**cla**·vo	**klah**-voh
rivet	el	re·**ma**·che	reh-**mah**-cheh
staple	la	**gra**·pa	**grah**-pah

© 2000 Kathy Parsons, Spanish for Cruisers

Sanding and grinding			
sandpaper	el	pa·**pel** de **li**·ja	pah-**pehl** deh **lee**-hah
sandpaper (wet sanding)	el	pa·**pel** de **li**·ja de **a**·gua	pah-**pehl** deh **lee**-hah deh ah-gwah
sanding disk	el	**dis**·co **pa**·ra li·ja·**do**·ra	**deess**-koh **pah**-rah lee-hah-**doh**-rah
sanding sheet for sander	la	**ho**·ja **pa**·ra li·ja·**do**·ra	oh-hah **pah**-rah lee-hah-**doh**-rah
grinding disk	el	**dis**·co **pa**·ra es·me·ri·**lar**	**deess**-koh **pah**-rah ehss-meh-ree-**lahr**
... coarse		**grue**·so	**grweh**-soh
... medium		me·**dia**·no	meh-**dyah**-noh
... fine		**fi**·no	**fee**-noh
valve grinding compound	la	**pas**·ta **pa**·ra es·me·ri·**lar** **vál**·vu·las	**pahss**-tah **pah**-rah ehs-meh-ree-**lahr** **vahl**-voo-lahss
padlock	el	can·**da**·do	kahn-**dah**-doh
key	la	**lla**·ve	**yah**-veh

Llave has many meanings: key, wrench, faucet, valve, switch
Llave de fondo is one way to say seacock.

... of stainless steel	... **de** a·**ce**·ro in·ox·i·**da**·ble	deh ah-**seh**-roh een-ok-ksee-**dah**-bleh
... of galvanized steel	... **de** a·**ce**·ro gal·va·ni·**za**·do	deh ah-**seh**-roh gahl-vah-nee-**sah**-doh
... of bronze	... **de** **bron**·ce	deh **brohn**-seh
... of aluminum	... **de** a·lu·**mi**·nio	deh ah-loo-**mee**-nyoh

© 2000 Kathy Parsons, Spanish for Cruisers

cable, wire	el	ca·ble	**kah**-bleh
wire (single)	el	a·**lam**·bre	ah-**lahm**-breh
3-conductor wire	el	**ca**·ble **de tres** con·duc·to·res	**kah**-bleh **deh trehss** kohn-dook-**toh**-rehss
power lead	el	**ca**·ble **de fuer**·za	**kah**-bleh **deh fwehr**-sah
gauge (of wire)	el	ca·**li**·bre	kah-**lee**-breh
# 12 wire	el	a·**lam**·bre **nú**·me·ro **do**·ce	ah-**lahm**-breh **noo**-meh-roh **doh**-seh
copper conductor	el	con·duc·**tor de co**·bre	kohn-dook-**tohr deh koh**-breh
bare wire	el	a·**lam**·bre des·**nu**·do	ah-**lahm**-breh dehss-**noo**-doh
solid wire	el	a·**lam**·bre **de un so**·lo **hi**·lo	ah-**lahm**-breh **deh oon soh**-loh **ee**-loh
stranded wire	el	a·**lam**·bre **con** ra·**ci**·mos	ah-**lahm**-breh **kohn** rah-**see**-mohss
insulation	el	ais·la·**mien**·to	eyess-lah-**myehn**-toh
insulator	el	ais·**lan**·te	eyess-**lahn**-teh
electric cord	el	cor·**dón**	kohr-**dohn**
coax cable	el	**ca**·ble co·a·**xial**	**kah**-bleh koh-ahk-**sial**
cover of cable	el	**for**·ro	**foh**-rroh
	la	ca·**mi**·sa	kah-**mee**-sah

© 2000 Kathy Parsons, Spanish for Cruisers

fuse	el	fusible	foo-**see**-bleh
30-amp fuse	el	fusible **de trein**ta am**pe**rios	foo-**see**-bleh **deh trayn**-tah ahm-**peh**-ryohss
alternating current (A/C)	la	corriente alterna	koh-**rryehn**-teh ahl-**tehr**-nah
direct current (D/C)	la	corriente directa	koh-**rryehn**-teh dee-**rehk**-tah
fuse holder	el	portafusibles	pohr-tah-foo-**see**-blehss
current rating	el	**pa**so de corriente	**pah**-soh deh koh-**rryehn**-teh
circuit breaker	el	**brea**ker	**breh**-ker
	el	interrup**tor** auto**má**tico	een-teh-rroop-**tohr** ow-toh-**mah**-tee-koh

plug	el	en**chu**fe	ehn-**choo**-feh
	la	cla**vi**ja	klah-**vee**-hah
three-pin plug	el	en**chu**fe **de tres po**los	ehn-**choo**-feh **deh trehss poh**-lohss
socket	el	**so**cket	**soh**-ket
	la	**toh**-mah	**toh**-mah
outlet	la	tomacorriente	toh-mah-koh-**rryehn**-teh
switch	el	**switch**	ehss-**weetch, swee**-cheh
	el	apaga**dor**	ah-pah-gah-**dohr**
	el	interrup**tor**	een-teh-rroop-**tohr**
	la	**lla**ve (with key)	**yah**-veh
	el	bo**tón** (button)	boh-**tohn**

© 2000 Kathy Parsons, Spanish for Cruisers

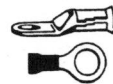 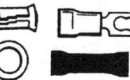        

Connectors

connection	la	co·ne·**xión**	koh-nehk-**syohn**
connector	el	co·nec·**tor** e·**léc**·tri·co	koh-nehk-**tohr** eh-**lehk**-tree-koh
terminal	el	ter·mi·**nal**	tehr-mee-**nahl**
ring terminal	el	ter·mi·**nal** de a·**ni**·llo	tehr-mee-**nahl** deh ah-**nee**-yoh
spade terminal	el	ter·mi·**nal** de hor·**qui**·lla	tehr-mee-**nahl** deh ohr-**kee**-yah
butt connector	el	en·**pal**·me de ex·**tre**·mos	ehn-**pahl**-meh deh ehkss-**treh**-mohss
electrical tape	la	**cin**·ta de ais·**lar**	**seen**-tah deh eyess-**lahr**
	el	**tei**·pe *(Venezuela "Spanglish")*	**tay**-peh
box	la	**ca**·ja	**kah**-hah
cable clip	la	**gra**·pa de **plás**·ti·co	**grah**-pah deh **plahss**-tee-koh
cable tie	la	a·**ma**·rra **pa**·ra **ca**·bles	ah-**mah**-rrah **pah**-rah **kah**-blehss
solder (rosin cored)	la	sol·da·**du**·ra (**con** ro·**si**·na)	sohl-dah-**doo**-rah (**kohn** roh-**see**-nah)
solid-wire solder	la	sol·da·**du**·ra de a·**lam**·bre **só**·li·do	sohl-dah-**doo**-rah deh ah-**lahm**-breh **soh**-lee-doh
lead-free *(without lead)*		... **sin** **plo**·mo	**seen** **ploh**-moh
soldering flux	el	fun·**den**·te **pa**·ra sol·**dar**	foon-**dehn**-teh **pah**-rah sohl-**dahr**

© 2000 Kathy Parsons, Spanish for Cruisers

Batteries

battery *(ship's battery)*	la	ba·te·**rí**·a	bah-teh-**ree**-ah
	el	a·cu·mu·la·**dor**	ah-koo-moo-lah-**dohr**
battery *(small D,C, AA, etc.)*	la	**pi**·la	**pee**-lah
9-volt battery	la	**pi**·la **de nue**·ve **vol**·tios	**pee**-lah **deh nweh**-veh **vohl**-tyohss
C, D, AA, AAA		C, D, **do**·ble A, **tri**·ple A	**Seh, Deh,** doh-bleh **Ah, tree**-pleh **Ah**
alkaline		al·ca·li·na	ahl-kah-lee-nah
nickel cadmium		**ní**·quel-**cad**·mio	**nee**-kehl **kahd**-myoh
battery charger	el	car·ga·**dor de** ba·te·**rí**·as	kahr-gah-**dohr deh** bah-teh-**ree**-ahss
bulb	el	**fo**·co	**foh**-koh
	la	bom·**bi**·lla	bohm-**bee**-yah

Volts, Amps, Watts

alternating current (A/C)	la	co·**rrien**·te al·**ter**·na	koh-**rryehn**-teh ahl-**tehr**-nah
direct current (D/C)	la	co·**rrien**·te di·**rec**·ta	koh-**rryehn**-teh dee-**rehk**-tah
	la	co·**rrien**·te con·**ti**·nua	koh-**rryehn**-teh kohn-**tee**-nwah
12 volts	los	**do**·ce **vol**·tios	**doh**-seh **vohl**-tyohss
24 volts	los	vein·ti·**cua**·tro **vol**·tios	vayn-tee-**kwah**-troh **vohl**-tyohss
120 volts	los	**cien**·to **vein**·te **vol**·tios	**syehn**-toh **vayn**-teh **vohl**-tyohss
amps	los	am·**pe**·rios	ahm-**peh**-ryohss
watts	los	**watts**	**wahts**

See also Electronic Components, page 156

© 2000 Kathy Parsons, Spanish for Cruisers

Fuel

fuel	el	com·bus·**ti**·ble	kohm-booss-**tee**-bleh
diesel	el	gas·**oil**	gahss-**oil**
	el	**die**·sel *(usually understood)*	**dee**-sehl
	el	pe·**tró**·le·o *(Cuba only)*	peh-**troh**-leh-oh
gasoline	la	ga·so·**li**·na *(not "gas"!)*	gah-soh-**lee**-nah
gasoline, unleaded	la	ga·so·**li**·na **sin plo**·mo	gah-soh-**lee**-nah **seen ploh**-moh
pre-mix (with 2-cycle oil)		**pre**-mez·**cla**·do	preh-mehss-**klah**-doh
propane	el	**gas** (pro·**pa**·no)	**gahss** (proh-**pah**-noh)
kerosene	el	ke·ro·**sén**	keh-roh-**sehn**
	el	pe·**tró**·le·o **de lám**·pa·ra	peh-**troh**-leh-oh **deh lahm**-pah-rah
	la	ga·so·**li**·na **blan**·ca *(white gas)*	gah-soh-**lee**-nah **blahn**-kah

Fluids

motor oil (for diesel motors)	el	a·**cei**·te de mo·**tor die**·sel	ah-**say**-teh **deh** moh-**tohr dee**-sehl
motor oil (for gasoline motors)	el	a·**cei**·te de mo·**tor** de ga·so·**li**·na	ah-**say**-teh **deh** moh-**tohr deh** gah-soh-**lee**-nah

© 2000 Kathy Parsons, Spanish for Cruisers

30 weight		.... de grado 30	deh grah-doh trayn-tah
40 weight		... de grado 40	deh grah-doh kwah-rehn-tah
multi-grade		multigrado	mool-tee-grah-doh
brand	la	marca	mahr-kah
two-cycle oil (outboard)	el	aceite de dos tiempos	ah-say-teh deh dohss tyehm-pohss
hydraulic fluid	el	aceite hidráulico	ah-say-teh ee-drow-lee-koh
transmission fluid	el	aceite de transmisión	ah-say-teh deh trahnss-mee-syohn
grease	la	grasa	grah-sah
gear case lube	el	lubricante para caja de cambios (... caja de velocidades)	loo-bree-kahn-teh pah-rah kah-hah deh kahm-byohss (...kah-hah deh veh-loh-see-dah-dehss)
antifreeze	el	anticongelante	ahn-tee-kohn-heh-lahn-teh
distilled water	el	agua destilada	ah-gwah dehss-tee-lah-dah
additive	el	aditivo	ah-dee-tee-voh
liter	el	litro	lee-troh
gallon	el	galón	gah-lohn

I need ...	Necesito ...	Neh-seh-see-toh ...
I want ... liters of ..	Quiero ... litros de ...	Kyeh-roh ... lee-trohss deh ...
Full, please.	Lleno, por favor.	Yeh-noh, pohr fah-vohr.
Enough!	Ya!	Yah!

© 2000 Kathy Parsons, Spanish for Cruisers

Filters

fuel filter	el	**fil**tro **de** combus·ti·ble	**feel**-troh **deh** kohm-booss-**tee**-bleh
oil filter	el	**fil**tro **de** a·**cei**te	**feel**-troh **deh** ah-**say**-teh
number	el	**nú**·me·ro ...	**noo**-meh-roh
filter element	el	e·le·**men**·to **de fil**·tro	eh-leh-**mehn**-toh **deh feel**-troh
cartridge	el	car·**tu**·cho	kahr-**too**-choh

Other

spark plug	la	bu·**jí**·a	boo-**hee**-ah
	la	can·**de**·la *(Central America)*	kahn-**deh**-lah
belt	la	co·**rre**·a *(Caribbean)*	koh-**rreh**-ah
	la	**ban**·da *(Mexico)*	**bahn**-dah
	la	**fa**·ja *(Guatemala)*	**fah**-hah
zinc anode	el	**á**·no·do **de zinc**	ah-noh-doh **deh seenk**
zinc pencil	el	**lá**·piz **de zinc**	**lah**-peess **deh seenk**
	el	**zinc** in·**ter**·no	**seenk** een-**tehr**-noh

© 2000 Kathy Parsons, Spanish for Cruisers

hose clamp	la	abrazadera	ah-brah-sah-**deh**-rah
impeller	el	impul**sor**	eem-pool-**sohr**
	el	impe**len**te	eem-peh-**lehn**-teh
packing for the stuffing box	la	empaqueta**du**ra **pa**ra **la** prensa·es**to**pas	ehm-pah-keh-tah-**doo**-rah **pah**-rah **lah** prehn-sah-ehss-**toh**-pahss
	el	empaque **pa**ra **el** es·to·**pe**ro *(Mexico)*	ehm-**pah**-keh **pah**-rah **ehl** ehss-toh-**peh**-roh

Sample sentences		
I need a spark plug number ...	Nece**si**to **u**na bu**jí**a **nú**me·ro ...	Neh-seh-**see**-toh oo-nah boo-**hee**-ah **noo**-meh-roh ...
The Champion number is ...	**El nú**me·ro **de** "**Cham**pion" **es** ...	**Ehl noo**-meh-roh **deh** "**Cham**-pion" **ehss** ...
Do you have stainless steel hose clamps?	¿**Tie**ne abraza**de**ras **de** a**ce**ro in·oxi**da**ble?	**Tyeh**-neh ah-brah-sah-**deh**-rahss **deh** ah-**seh**-roh een-oh-ksee-**dah**-bleh?
Are they stainless steel?	¿**Son de** a**ce**ro in·oxi**da**ble?	**Sohn deh** ah-**seh**-roh een-oh-ksee-**dah**-bleh?
Where can I buy ...?	¿**Dón**de **pue**do com**prar** ...?	**Dohn**-deh **pweh**-doh kohm-**prahr** ...?

© 2000 Kathy Parsons, Spanish for Cruisers

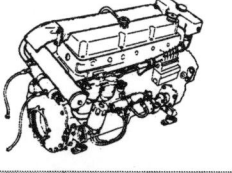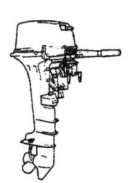

English		Spanish	Pronunciation
engine, motor	el	**mo·tor**	moh-**tohr**
type of engine, motor	el	**ti·**po **de** mo·tor	**tee**-poh **deh** moh-**tohr**
diesel engine	el	mo·**tor die·**sel	moh-**tohr dee**-sehl
gas engine	el	mo·**tor de** ga·so·li·na	moh-**tohr deh** gah-soh-**lee**-nah
outboard motor	el	fue·ra·**bor·**da	fweh-rah-**bohr**-dah
	el	mo·**tor fue·**ra **de bor·**da	moh-**tohr fweh**-rah **deh bohr**-dah
generator	el	ge·ne·ra·**dor**	heh-neh-rah-**dohr**
inboard		in·tra·**bor·**da	een-trah-**bohr**-dah
		den·tro **de bor·**da	**dehn**-troh **deh bohr**-dah
outboard		fue·ra·**bor·**da	fweh-rah-**bohr**-dah
		fue·ra **de bor·**da	**fweh**-rah **deh bohr**-dah
horsepower	los	ca·**ba·**llos	kah-**bah**-yohss
number of cylinders	el	**nú·**me·ro **de** ci·**lin·**dros	**noo**-meh-roh **deh** see-leen-drohss
two cylinder		**de dos** ci·**lin·**dros	**deh dohss** see-leen-drohss
two-stroke, two-cycle		**de dos tiem·**pos	**deh dohss tyehm**-pohss
four-stroke, four-cycle		**de cua·**tro **tiem·**pos	**deh kwah**-troh **tyehm**-pohss

© 2000 Kathy Parsons, Spanish for Cruisers

cubic capacity	la	cilin**dra**da	see-leen-**drah**-dah
displacement	el	despla·za**mien**to	dess-plah-sah-**myehn**-toh

with turbocharger	**con** tur·bo·car·ga·**dor**		**kohn** toor-boh-kahr-gah-**dohr**
fresh-water cooled	en·**fria**·do **por** a·gua **dul**·ce		ehn-**fryah**-doh **pohr** ah-gwah **dool**-seh
salt-water cooled	en·**fria**·do **por** a·gua sa·**la**·da		ehn-**fryah**-doh **pohr** ah-gwah sah-**lah**-dah

short shaft *(outboard)*	la	**co**·la **cor**·ta	**koh**-lah **kohr**-tah
	la	**pa**·ta **cor**·ta	**pah**-tah **kohr**-tah
long shaft	la	**co**·la **lar**·ga	**koh**-lah **lahr**-gah
	la	**pa**·ta **lar**·ga	**pah**-tah **lahr**-gah

brand or make of motor	la	**mar**·ca	**mahr**-kah
model number	el	**nú**·me·ro **del** mo·**de**·lo	**noo**-meh-roh **dehl** moh-**deh**-loh
serial number	el	**nú**·me·ro **de** se·rie	**noo**-meh-roh **deh seh**-ryeh
part number	el	**nú**·me·ro **de la pie**·za	**noo**-meh-roh **deh lah pyeh**-sah
specifications	las	es·pe·ci·fi·ca·**cio**·nes	ehss-peh-see-fee-kah-**syoh**-nehss
year	el	**a**·ño	**ah**-nyoh
engine hours	las	**ho**·ras **de** mo·**tor**	**oh**-rahss **deh** moh-**tohr**
	las	**ho**·ras **de** tra·**ba**·jo	**oh**-rahss **deh** trah-**bah**-hoh

© 2000 Kathy Parsons, Spanish for Cruisers

English		Spanish	Pronunciation
back pressure	la	contra·pre**sión**	kohn-trah-preh-**syohn**
clearance, gap, opening	la	a·ber**·tu**·ra	ah-behr-**too**-rah
combustion	la	com·bus**·tión**	kohm-booss-**tyohn**
compression	la	com·pre**·sión**	kohm-preh-**syohn**
compression ratio	la	re·la**·ción** de com·pre**·sión**	reh-lah-**syohn** deh kohm-preh-**syohn**
exhaust	el	es**·ca**·pe	ehss-**kah**-peh
friction	la	fric**·ción**	freek-**syohn**
hours	las	**ho**·ras	**oh**-rahss
ignition order	el	**or**·den de en·cen**·di**·do	**ohr**-dehn deh ehn-sehn-**dee**-doh
ignition timing	el	**tiem**·po de en·cen**·di**·do	**tyehm**-poh deh ehn-sehn-**dee**-doh
intake	la	ad·mi**·sión**	ahd-mee-**syohn**
play	el	**jue**·go	**hweh**-goh
power	la	**fuer**·za	**fwehr**-sah
	la	po**·ten**·cia	poh-**tehn**-syah
ratio	la	re·la**·ción**	reh-lah-**syohn**
revolutions	las	re·vo·lu**·cio**·nes	reh-voh-loo-**syoh**-nehss
rotation	la	ro·ta**·ción**	roh-tah-**syohn**
speed	la	ve·lo·ci**·dad**	veh-loh-see-**dahd**
suction	la	as·pi·ra**·ción**	ahss-pee-rah-**syohn**
tolerance	la	to·le**·ren**·cia	toh-leh-**rehn**-syah
torque	la	**fuer**·za de tor**·sión**	**fwehr**-sah deh tohr-**syohn**

© 2000 Kathy Parsons, Spanish for Cruisers

inspection	la	revisión	reh-vee-**syohn**
overhaul	la	reconstrucción	reh-kohn-strook-**syohn**
adjustment	el	ajuste	ah-**hooss**-teh
tune-up	la	afinación	ah-fee-nah-**syohn**
alignment	la	alineación	ah-lee-neh-ah-**syohn**
decarbonizing	la	descarbonización	dehss-kahr-boh-nee-sah-**syohn**
reconditioning	el	reacondicionamiento	reh-ah-kohn-dee-syoh-nah-**myehn**-toh
test	la	**prue**ba	**prweh**-bah
corrosion	la	corrosión	koh-rroh-**syohn**
leak	la	**fu**ga	**foo**-gah
misfire	el	**fa**llo **de** encen**di**do	**fah**-yoh **deh** ehn-sehn-**dee**-doh
noise	el	**rui**do	**rwee**-doh
smoke	el	**hu**mo	**oo**-moh
vibration	la	vibra**ción**	vee-brah-**syohn**
wear	el	des**gas**te	dehss-**gahss**-teh
Can you check ...?	¿**Pue**de revi**sar** ...? ¿**Pue**de cheque**ar** ...?		**Pweh**-deh reh-vee-**sahr** ...? **Pweh**-deh cheh-keh-**ahr** ...?
Can you adjust ...?	¿**Pue**de ajus**tar** ...?		**Pweh**-deh ah-hooss-**tahr** ...?
Can you tune-up ...?	¿**Pue**de afi**nar** ...?		**Pweh**-deh ah-fee-**nahr** ...?

© 2000 Kathy Parsons, Spanish for Cruisers

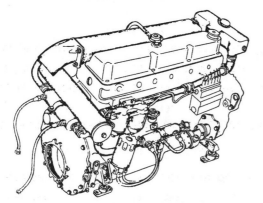 

cylinder block	el	**blo**que (**de** ci·**lin**·dros)	**bloh-keh** (**deh** see-**leen**-drohss)
	el	**bloc**	**blok**
crankcase	el	**cár**·ter	**kahr**-tehr
cylinder head	la	cu·**la**·ta	koo-**lah**-tah
	la	ca·**be**·za *(Mexico)*	kah-**beh**-sah
head gasket	la	**jun**·ta **de** cu·**la**·ta	**hoon**-tah **deh** koo-**lah**-tah
	la	**jun**·ta **de la** ca·**be**·za *(Mexico)*	**hoon**-tah **deh lah** kah-**beh**-sah
cylinder	el	ci·**lin**·dro	see-**leen**-droh
liner	la	ca·**mi**·sa	kah-**mee**-sah

© 2000 Kathy Parsons, Spanish for Cruisers

piston	el	**pis**·**tón**	peess-**tohn**
skirt (piston)	la	**fal**·da (**del** pis·**tón**)	**fahl**-dah **dehl** peess-**tohn**
groove	la	ra·**nu**·ra	rah-**noo**-rah
piston pin	el	pa·sa·**dor del** pis·**tón**	pah-sah-**dohr dehl** peess-**tohn**
snap ring	el	re·te·ne·**dor**	reh-teh-neh-**dohr**
	el	se·**gu**·ro **de** re·**sor**·te	seh-**goo**-roh **deh** reh-**sohr**-teh
piston ring	el	**a**·ro **del** pis·**tón**	**ah**-roh **dehl** pees-**tohn**
	el	a·**ni**·llo **del** pis·**tón**	ah-**nee**-yoh **dehl** pees-**tohn**
compression ring	el	**a**·ro **de** com·pre·**sión**	**ah**-roh **deh** kohm-preh-**syohn**
oil control ring	el	**a**·ro ras·ca·**dor de** a·**cei**·te	**ah**-roh rahss-kah-**dohr deh** ah-**say**-teh
connecting rod	la	**bie**·la	**byeh**-lah
rod big end bearing	el	co·ji·**ne**·te **de** ca·**be**·za **de bie**·la	koh-hee-**neh**-teh **deh** kah-**beh**-sah **deh** **byeh**-lah
bolt	el	tor·**ni**·llo	tohr-**nee**-yoh
There's a leak at the head gasket.		**Hay** u·na **fu**·ga **en la jun**·ta **de la** cu·**la**·ta.	**Eye** oo-nah **foo**-gah **ehn lah hoon**-tah **deh lah** kah-**beh**-sah.
The engine was rebuilt ...		**El** mo·**tor fue** re·con·**strui**·do ...	**Ehl** moh-**tohr fweh** reh-kohn-**strwee**-doh ...
... 2 years ago.		**... ha**·ce **dos a**·ños.	... ah-**seh dohss** ah-nyohss.
... 500 engine hours ago.		**... ha**·ce qui·**nien**·tos **ho**·ras **de** mo·**tor**.	... ah-**seh** kee-**nyehn**-tohss oh-rahss **deh** moh-**tohr**.

© 2000 Kathy Parsons, Spanish for Cruisers

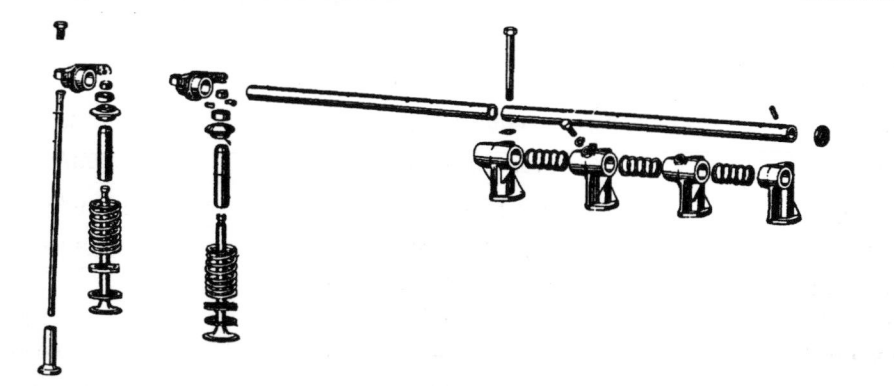

valve	la	**vál**·vu·la	**vahl**-voo-lah
intake valve	la	**vál**·vu·la **de** ad·mi·**sión**	**vahl**-voo-lah **deh** ahd-mee-**syohn**
exhaust valve	la	**vál**·vu·la **de** es·**ca**·pe	**vahl**-voo-lah **deh** ehss-**kah**-peh
valve guide	la	**guí**·a	**ghee**-ah
valve seat	el	a·**sien**·to	ah-**syehn**-toh
valve spring	el	re·**sor**·te **de vál**·vu·la	reh-**sohr**-teh **deh vahl**-voo-lah
lifter	el	le·van·ta·**vál**·vu·las	leh-vahn-tah-**vahl**-voo-lahss
	el	si·gue·**le**·va	see-gheh-**leh**-vah
pushrod	la	va·**ri**·lla **de** em·**pu**·je	vah-**ree**-yah **deh** ehm-**poo**-heh
rocker arm	el	ba·lan·**cín**	bah-lahn-**seen**

© 2000 Kathy Parsons, Spanish for Cruisers

crankshaft	el	ci·güe·**ñal**	see-gweh-**nyahl**
crankshaft bearing	el	co·ji·**ne**·te	koh-hee-**neh**-teh
	el	me·**tal**	meh-**tahl**
main bearing	el	co·ji·**ne**·te prin·ci·**pal**	koh-hee-**neh**-teh preen-see-**pahl**
	el	ba·**le**·ro prin·ci·**pal** *(Mexico)*	bah-**leh**-roh preen-see-**pahl**
timing chain	la	ca·**de**·na **de** dis·tri·bu·**ción**	kah-**deh**-nah **deh** deess-tree-boo-**syohn**
gear	el	pi·**ñon**	pee-**nyohn**
	el	en·gra·**na**·je	ehn-grah-**nah**-heh
	el	en·**gra**·ne	ehn-**grah**-neh
crankshaft oil seal	el	re·**tén de** a·**cei**·te **del** ci·güe·**ñal**	reh-**tehn deh** ah-**say**-teh **dehl** see-gweh-**nyahl**
rear seal	el	**se**·llo tra·**se**·ro	**seh**-yoh trah-**seh**-roh
	el	re·**tén** tra·**se**·ro	reh-**tehn** trah-**seh**-roh
flywheel	el	vo·**lan**·te	voh-**lahn**-teh
pulley	la	po·**le**·a	poh-**leh**-ah
belt	la	co·**rre**·a	koh-**rreh**-ah
	la	**ban**·da *(Mexico)*	**bahn**-dah
sprocket	la	**rue**·da den·**ta**·da	**rweh**-dah dehn-**tah**-dah
timing marks	las	**mar**·cas **de tiem**·po	**mahr**-kahss **deh tyehm**-poh
camshaft	el	**ár**·bol **de le**·vas	**ahr**-bohl **deh** leh-**vahss**
bearing	el	co·ji·**ne**·te	koh-hee-**neh**-teh
gear	el	pi·**ñon**	pee-**nyohn**
	el	en·**gra**·ne	ehn-**grah**-neh

© 2000 Kathy Parsons, Spanish for Cruisers

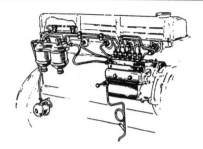

injectors	los	inyectores	een-yehk-**toh**-rehss
injection pump	la	**bom**·ba **de** inyec**ción**	**bohm**-bah **deh** een-yehk-**syohn**
input shaft	el	**e**·je pri**ma**·rio	**eh**-heh pree-**mah**-ryoh
	la	**fle**·cha pri**ma**·ria *(Mexico)*	**fleh**-chah pree-**mah**-ryah
injector tip, nozzle	el	inyec**tor**	een-yehk-**tohr**
pressure pipe	el	**tu**·bo **de** pre**sión**	**too**-boh **deh** preh-**syohn**
return pipe	el	**tu**·bo **de** re**tor**·no	**too**-boh **deh** reh-**tohr**-noh
governor	el	re·gu·la·**dor**	reh-goo-lah-**dohr**

fuel	el	com·bus·**ti**·ble	kohm-booss-**tee**-bleh
fuel lift pump (diesel)	la	**bom**·ba **de** gas·**oil** (**die**·sel)	**bohm**-bah **deh** gahss-**oil** (**dee**-sehl)
fuel lift pump (gasoline)	la	**bom**·ba **de** ga·so·**li**·na	**bohm**-bah **deh** gah-soh-**lee**-nah
fuel transfer pump	la	**bom**·ba **de** trans·fe·**ren**·cia **de** com·bus·**ti**·ble	**bohm**-bah **deh** trahnss-feh-**rehn**-syah **deh** kohm-booss-**tee**-bleh

© 2000 Kathy Parsons, Spanish for Cruisers

fuel lines	los la	**tu**·bos **de** com·bus·**ti**·ble tu·be·**rí**·a **de** a·li·men·ta·**ción**	**too**-bohss **deh** kohm-booss-**tee**-bleh too-beh-**ree**-ah **deh** ah-lee-mehn-tah-**syohn**
fuel hose	la	man·**gue**·ra **de** com·bus·ti·ble	mahn-**gheh**-rah **deh** kohm-boos-tee-bleh
high-pressure line	el	**tu**·bo **de** al·ta pre·**sión**	**too**-boh **deh** ahl-tah preh-**syohn**
low-pressure line	el	**tu**·bo **de** ba·ja pre·**sión**	**too**-boh **deh** bah-hah preh-**syohn**
fuel filter	el	**fil**·tro **de** com·bus·ti·ble	**feel**-troh **deh** kohm-booss-tee-bleh
water separator	el	se·pa·ra·**dor de** a·gua	seh-pah-rah-**dohr deh** ah-gwah
element	el	e·le·**men**·to	eh-leh-**mehn**-toh
fuel supply	el	su·mi·**nis**·tro **de** com·bus·ti·ble	soo-mee-**neess**-troh **deh** kohm-boos-**tee**-bleh
fuel shut-off valve	la	**vál**·vu·la **de** cie·rre **de** com·bus·ti·ble	**vahl**-voo-lah **deh** syeh-rreh **deh** kohm-booss-**tee**-bleh
fuel tank	el	**tan**·que **de** com·bus·ti·ble	**tahn**-keh **deh** kohm-booss-**tee**-bleh
fuel fill	la	**to**·ma **de** com·bus·ti·ble	**toh**-mah **deh** kohm-booss-**tee**-bleh
screen	la	**ma**·lla	**mah**-yah
bleed screw	el	tor·**ni**·llo **de pur**·ga	tohr-**nee**-yoh **deh poor**-gah
The fuel is dirty.		**El** com·bus·ti·ble es·**tá su**·cio.	**Ehl** kohm-booss-**tee**-bleh ehss-**tah soo**-syoh.
There is water in the fuel.		**Hay** a·gua **en el** com·bus·ti·ble.	**Eye** ah-gwah **ehn ehl** kohm-booss-**tee**-bleh.
The engine is flooded.		**El** mo·**tor** es·**tá** a·ho·**ga**·do.	**Ehl** moh-**tohr** ehss-**tah** ah-oh-**gah**-doh.
There is air in the fuel system.		**Hay ai**·re **en el** sis·te·ma **de** com·bus·ti·ble.	**Eye eye**-reh **ehn ehl** seess-**teh**-mah **deh** kohm-booss-**tee**-bleh.

© 2000 Kathy Parsons, Spanish for Cruisers

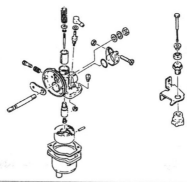

carburetor	el	carburador	kahr-boo-rah-**dohr**
float	el	flotador	floh-tah-**dohr**
float chamber	la	**cá**mara **del** flotador	**kah**-mah-rah **dehl** floh-tah-**dohr**
	la	**cu**ba **del** flotador	**koo**-bah **dehl** floh-tah-**dohr**
jet	la	es**pre**a	ehss-**preh**-ah
	el	surtidor	soor-tee-**dohr**
	el	chi**clé** (Cuba)	chee-**kleh**
main jet	la	es**pre**a princi**pal**	ehss-**preh**-ah preen-see-**pahl**
idle, slow-speed, pilot jet	la	es**pre**a **de ba**ja	ehss-**preh**-ah **deh bah**-hah
high speed jet	la	es**pre**a **de al**ta	ehss-**preh**-ah **deh ahl**-tah
check valve	la	**vál**vula **check**	**vahl**-voo-lah **chehk**
	la	**vál**vula anti-re**tor**no	**vahl**-voo-lah ahn-tee-reh-**tohr**-noh

© 2000 Kathy Parsons, Spanish for Cruisers

nozzle	el	pul·ve·ri·za·**dor**	pool-veh-ree-sah-**dohr**
	el	in·yec·**tor**	een-yehk-**tohr**
needle valve	la	**vál**·vu·la **de** a·**gu**·ja	**vahl**-voo-lah **deh** ah-**goo**-hah
seat (valve)	el	a·**sien**·to (**de la vál**·vu·la)	ah-**syehn**-toh (**deh lah vahl**-voo-lah)
butterfly valve	la	**vál**·vu·la **de la** ma·ri·**po**·sa	**vahl**-voo-lah **deh lah** mah-ree-**poh**-sah
gasket	la	**jun**·ta	**hoon**-tah
	el	em·**pa**·que (*Mexico*)	ehm-**pah**-keh
	la	em·pa·ca·**du**·ra (*Venezuela*)	ehm-pah-kah-**doo**-rah
diaphragm	el	dia·**frag**·ma	dyah-**frahg**-mah
choke	el	a·ho·ga·**dor**	ah-oh-gah-**dohr**
	el	es·tran·gu·la·**dor**	ehss-trahn-goo-lah-**dohr**
	el	**star**·ter	ehss-**tahr**-tehr

The carburetor is ...	**El** car·bu·ra·**dor** es·**tá** ...	**Ehl** kahr-boo-rah-**dohr** ehss-**tah** ...
... flooded.	... a·ho·**ga**·do.	... ah-oh-**gah**-doh.
...dirty.	... **su**·cio.	... **soo**-syoh.

Can you ...?	¿**Pue**·de ...?	**Pweh**-deh ...?
... clean the carburetor	... lim·**piar el** car·bu·ra·**dor**	... leem-**pyahr ehl** kahr-boo-rah-**dohr**
... rebuild the carburetor	... re·con·**struir el** car·bu·ra·**dor**	... reh-kohn-stroo-**eer ehl** kahr-boo-rah-**dohr**
... adjust the carburetor	... a·jus·**tar el** car·bu·ra·**dor**	... ah-hooss-**tahr ehl** kahr-boo-rah-**dohr**

© 2000 Kathy Parsons, Spanish for Cruisers

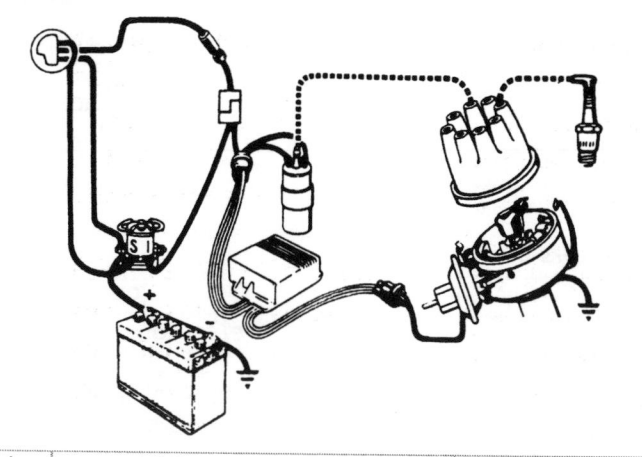

ignition	el	en·cen·di·do	ehn-sehn-**dee**-doh
electronic ignition	el	en·cen·**di**·do e·lec·**tró**·ni·co	ehn-sehn-**dee**-doh eh-lehk-**troh**-nee-koh
ignition module	el	**mó**·du·lo **de** en·cen·di·do	**moh**-doo-loh **deh** ehn-sehn-**dee**-doh
distributor	el	dis·tri·bui·**dor**	deess-tree-bwee-**dohr**
magneto	el	mag·**ne**·to	mahg-**neh**-toh
rotor	el	ro·**tor**	roh-**tohr**
ignition coil	la	bo·**bi**·na **de** en·cen·di·do	boh-**bee**-nah **deh** ehn-sehn-**dee**-doh
condenser	el	con·den·sa·**dor**	kohn-dehn-sah-**dohr**

© 2000 Kathy Parsons, Spanish for Cruisers

pickup coil	la	bo·**bi**·na cap·ta·**do**·ra	boh-**bee**-nah kahp-tah-**doh**-rah
points	los los	pla·**ti**·nos con·**tac**·tos	plah-**tee**-nohss kohn-**tahk**-tohss
spark plug	la la	bu·**jí**·a can·**de**·la (Guatemala)	boo-**hee**-ah kahn-**deh**-lah
spark plug gap	la	a·ber·**tu**·ra **de las** bu·**jí**·as	ah-behr-**too**-rah **deh lahss** boo-**hee**-ahss
spark	la	**chis**·pa	**cheess**-pah
spark plug lead	el	**ca**·ble **de la** bu·**jí**·a	**kah**-bleh **deh lah** boo-**hee**-ah

Spark plug problems

It doesn't spark.	**No tie**·ne **chis**·pa.	Noh **tyeh**-neh **cheess**-pah.
The spark plug is burned.	**La** bu·**jí**·a es·**tá** que·**ma**·da.	Lah boo-**hee**-ah ehss-**tah** keh-**mah**-dah.
The spark plug is wet.	**La** bu·**jí**·a es·**tá** mo·**ja**·da.	Lah boo-**hee**-ah ehss-**tah** moh-**hah**-dah.
The spark plug is carbonned.	**La** bu·**jí**·a es·**tá** car·bo·ni·**za**·da.	Lah boo-**hee**-ah ehss-**tah** kahr-boh-nee-**sah**-dah.
Can you check ...?	¿**Pue**·de re·vi·**sar** ...?	Pweh-deh reh-vee-**sahr** ...?
Can you adjust ...?	¿**Pue**·de a·jus·**tar** ...?	Pweh-deh ah-hooss-**tahr** ...?
Can you replace ...?	¿**Pue**·de cam·**biar** ...?	Pweh-deh kahm-**byahr** ...?
Can you tune-up ...?	¿**Pue**·de a·fi·**nar** ...?	Pweh-deh ah-fee-**nahr** ...?
Can you clean ...?	¿**Pue**·de lim·**piar** ...?	Pweh-deh leem-**pyahr** ...?

© 2000 Kathy Parsons, Spanish for Cruisers

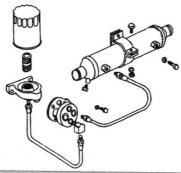

lubrication	el	en·**gra**·se	ehn-**grah**-seh
motor oil	el	a·**cei**·te (**de** mo·**tor**)	ah-**say**-teh (**deh** moh-**tohr**)
dipstick	la	va·**ri**·lla **del** ni·**vel de** a·cei·te	vah-**ree**-yah **dehl** nee-**vehl deh** ah-**say**-teh
oil-filler cap	el	ta·**pón de tan**·que **de** a·cei·te	tah-**pohn deh tahn**-keh **deh** ah-**say**-teh
oil filter	el	**fil**·tro **de** a·**cei**·te	**feel**-troh **deh** ah-**say**-teh
oil pressure sender	el	sen·**sor de la** pre·**sión del** a·cei·te	sehn-**sohr deh lah** preh-**syohn dehl** ah-**say**-teh
	el	**bul**·bo **de la** pre·**sión** ...	**bool**-boh **deh lah** preh-**syohn** ...
oil pressure gauge	el	in·di·ca·**dor de la** pre·**sión del** a·cei·te	een-dee-kah-**dohr deh lah** preh-**syohn deh** ah-**say**-teh
	el	ma·**nó**·me·tro **de la** pre·**sión del** a·cei·te	mah-**noh**-meh-troh **deh lah** preh-**syohn deh** ah-**say**-teh
oil drain plug	el	ta·**pón de** dre·**na**·je **de** a·cei·te	tah-**pohn deh** dreh-**nah**-heh **deh** ah-**say**-teh

© 2000 Kathy Parsons, Spanish for Cruisers

breather	el	respirador	rehss-pee-rah-**dohr**
oil pump	la	**bom**ba **de** a·**cei**·te	**bohm**-bah **deh** ah-**say**-teh
oil seal	el	re·**tén** **de** a·**cei**·te	reh-**tehn** **deh** ah-**say**-teh
	el	**se**·llo **de** a·**cei**·te	**seh**-yoh **deh** ah-**say**-teh
	la	es·to·**pe**·ra *(Venezuela)*	ehss-toh-**peh**-rah
pressure relief valve	la	**vál**·vu·la a·li·via·**do**·ra	**vahl**-voo-lah ah-lee-vyah-**doh**-rah
oil sump, pan	el	**cár**·ter	**kahr**-tehr
strainer	la	co·la·**de**·ra	koh-lah-**deh**-rah
low oil pressure	la	pre·**sión** **del** a·**cei**·te **ba**·ja	preh-**syohn** **dehl** ah-**say**-teh **bah**-hah
Can you ...?		¿**Pue**·de ...?	**Pweh**-deh ...?
... check the oil level		... re·vi·**sar** **el** ni·**vel** **de** a·**cei**·te	... reh-vee-**sahr** **ehl** nee-**vehl** **deh** ah-**say**-teh
... add oil		... e·**char** a·**cei**·te	... eh-**chahr** ah-**say**-teh
... change the oil and filter		... cam·**biar** **el** a·**cei**·te **y** **el** **fil**·tro	... kahm-**byahr** **ehl** ah-**say**-teh **ee** **ehl** **feel**-troh
... to drain the oil		... va·**ciar** **el** a·**cei**·te	... vah-**syahr** **ehl** ah-**say**-teh
air intake	la	ad·mi·**sión** **de** **ai**·re	ahd-mee-**syohn** **deh** **eye**-reh
	la	**to**·ma **de** **ai**·re	**toh**-mah **deh** **eye**-reh
intake manifold	el	**múl**·ti·ple **de** ad·mi·**sión**	**mool**-tee-pleh **deh** ahd-mee-**syohn**
air filter or cleaner	el	**fil**·tro **de** **ai**·re	**feel**-troh **deh** **eye**-reh

© 2000 Kathy Parsons, Spanish for Cruisers

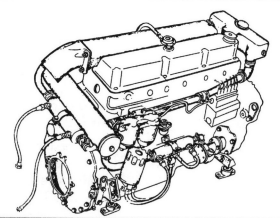

cooling	el	en·fria·**mien**·to	ehn-fryah-**myehn**-toh
seacock	el	**gri**·fo **de fon**·do	**gree**-foh **deh fohn**-doh
	la	**lla**·ve **de fon**·do	**yah**-veh **deh fohn**-doh
	la	**vál**·vu·la **de fon**·do	**vahl**-voo-lah **deh fohn**-doh
	la	**to**·ma **de fon**·do	**toh**-mah **deh fohn**-doh
water strainer	la	co·la·**de**·ra **de a**·gua	koh-lah-**deh**-rah **deh ah**-gwah
	el	**fil**·tro **de a**·gua	**feel**-troh **deh ah**-gwah
hose	la	man·**gue**·ra	mahn-**gheh**-rah
hose clamp	la	a·bra·za·**de**·ra	ah-brah-sah-**deh**-rah
expansion tank	el	**tan**·que **de** ex·pan·**sión**	**tahn**-keh **deh** ehkss-pahn-**syohn**
water filler cap	el	ta·**pón pa**·ra **tan**·que **de a**·gua	tah-**pohn pah**-rah **tahn**-keh **deh ah**-gwah

© 2000 Kathy Parsons, Spanish for Cruisers

thermostat	el	termostato	tehr-mohss-**tah**-toh
waterjacket	la	camisa	kah-**mee**-sah
heat exchanger	el	intercambiador de calor	een-tehr-kahm-byah-**dohr** deh kah-**lohr**
zinc anode	el	**ánodo de zinc**	**ah**-noh-doh **deh seenk**
distilled water	el	**a**gua destilada	**ah**-gwah dehss-tee-lah-dah
antifreeze	el	anticongelante	ahn-tee-kohn-heh-**lahn**-teh
strainer	la	coladerа	koh-lah-**deh**-rah
exhaust	**el**	escape	ehss-kah-peh
exhaust manifold	el	**múltiple de escape**	**mool**-tee-pleh **deh** ehss-kah-peh
exhaust pipe	el	**tubo de escape**	**too**-boh **deh** ehss-kah-peh
exhaust hose	la	man**gue**ra de escape	mahn-**gheh**-rah **deh** ehss-kah-peh
exhaust valve	la	**vál**vula de escape	**vahl**-voo-lah **deh** ehss-kah-peh
exhaust elbow	el	**co**do de escape	**koh**-doh **deh** ehss-kah-peh
exhaust fumes	los	**ga**ses de escape	**gah**-sehss **deh** ehss-kah-peh
muffler, silencer	el	silenciador	see-lehn-syah-**dohr**
pyrometer	el	pirómetro	pee-**roh**-meh-troh
The hose is plugged up.		**La** man**gue**ra es**tá** tapada.	**Lah** mahn-**gheh**-rah ehss-**tah** tah-**pah**-dah.
The engine overheats.		**El** motor se recalienta.	**Ehl** moh-**tohr** seh reh-kah-**lyen**-tah.
No exhaust water is coming out.		**No** sale agua de escape.	**Noh** sah-leh ah-gwah **deh** ehss-kah-peh.

© 2000 Kathy Parsons, Spanish for Cruisers

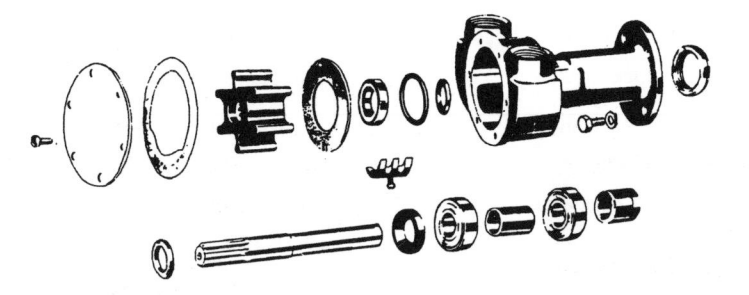

water pump	la	**bom**ba **de a**gua	**bohm**-bah **deh** ah-gwah
fresh water pump	la	**bom**ba **de a**gua **dul**ce	**bohm**-bah **deh** ah-gwah **dool**-seh
raw water pump	la	**bom**ba **de a**gua sa·la·da	**bohm**-bah **deh** ah-gwah sah-**lah**-dah
centrifugal pump	la	**bom**ba cen·**trí**fu·ga	**bohm**-bah sehn-**tree**-foo-gah
bearing	el	co·ji·**ne**·te	koh-hee-**neh**-teh
	el	ba·**le**·ro *(Mexico)*	bah-**leh**-roh
cam	la	**le**·va	**leh**-vah
cover	la	**ta**·pa	**tah**-pah
gasket	la	**jun**·ta	**hoon**-tah
	el	em·**pa**·que *(Mexico)*	ehm-**pah**-keh
	la	em·pa·ca·**du**·ra *(Venezuela)*	ehm-pah-kah-**doo**-rah
housing	la	car·**ca**·sa	kahr-**kah**-sah

© 2000 Kathy Parsons, Spanish for Cruisers

seal *(water)*	el	re·**tén** (**de a**·gua)	reh-**tehn** (**deh ah**-gwah)
	el	**se**·llo (**de a**·gua)	**seh**-yoh (**deh ah**-gwah)
	la	es·to·**pe**·ra (**de a**·gua) *(Venezuela)*	ehss-toh-**peh**-rah (**deh ah**-gwah)
shaft	el	**e**·je	**eh**-heh
	la	**fle**·cha *(Mexico)*	**fleh**-chah
seal *(oil)*	el	re·**tén** (**de a**·**cei**·te)	reh-**tehn** (**deh ah**-**say**-teh)
	el	**se**·llo (**de a**·**cei**·te)	**seh**-yoh (**deh ah**-**say**-teh)
	la	es·to·**pe**·ra (**de a**·**cei**·te) *(Venezuela)*	ehss-toh-**peh**-rah (**deh ah**-**say**-teh)
vane *(centrifugal pump)*	la	a·**le**·ta	ah-**leh**-tah
belt	la	co·**rre**·a	koh-**rreh**-ah
	la	**ban**·da *(Mexico)*	**bahn**-dah
pulley	la	po·**le**·a	poh-**leh**-ah
hose	la	man·**gue**·ra	mahn-**gheh**-rah
impeller	el	im·pul·**sor**	eem-pool-**sohr**
	el	im·pe·**len**·te	eem-peh-**lehn**-teh

The engine overheats.	**El** mo·**tor se** re·ca·**lien**·ta.	**Ehl** moh-**tohr seh** reh-kah-**lyehn**-tah.
No exhaust water comes out.	**No sa**·le **a**·gua **del** es·**ca**·pe.	**Noh** sah-leh **ah**-gwah **dehl** ehss-**kah**-peh.
Little exhaust water comes out.	**Sa**·le **po**·ca **a**·gua **del** es·**ca**·pe.	**Sah**-leh **poh**-kah **ah**-gwah **dehl** ehss-**kah**-peh.

© 2000 Kathy Parsons, Spanish for Cruisers

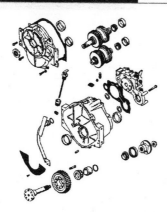
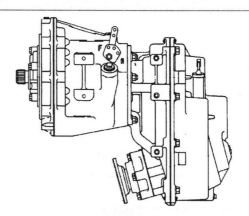

transmission	la	trans·mi·**sión**	trahnss-mee-**syohn**
gearbox	la	**ca**·ja **de cam**·bios	kah-hah **deh kahm**-byohss
... hydraulic		... hi·**dráu**·li·ca	... ee-**drow**-lee-kah
... automatic		... au·to·**má**·ti·ca	... ow-toh-**mah**-tee-kah
... manual		... ma·**nual**	... mah-**nwahl**
... direct		... di·**rec**·ta	... dee-**rehk**-tah
in-line		... **en lí**·ne·a	... **ehn** lee-neh-ah
v-drive	la	trans·mi·**sión en V**	trahnss-mee-**syohn ehn veh**

© 2000 Kathy Parsons, Spanish for Cruisers

reduction	la	reduc**ción**	reh-dook-**syohn**
ratio	la	rela**ción**	reh-lah-**syohn**
2:1 ratio	la	rela**ción de dos a u**no	reh-lah-**syohn deh dohss ah oo**-noh
forward		adelante	ah-deh-**lahn**-teh
reverse		re**ver**sa	reh-**vehr**-sah
neutral (gear)		neu**tral**	neh-oo-**trahl**
		punto **muer**to	**poon**-toh **mwehr**-toh
gear	el	en**gra**ne	ehn-**grah**-neh
	el	engra**na**je	ehn-grah-**nah**-heh
gears, speeds	los	**cam**bios	**kahm**-byohss
	las	veloci**da**des	veh-loh-see-**dah**-dehss
planetary gear	el	en**gra**ne plane**ta**rio	ehn-**grah**-neh plah-neh-**tah**-ryoh
pinion, gear wheel	el	pi**ñon**	pee-**nyohn**
	la	**rue**da den**ta**da	**rweh**-dah dehn-**tah**-dah
ring gear	el	a**ri**llo den**ta**do	ah-**ree**-yoh dehn-**tah**-doh
clutch	el	**clutch**	**klohch**
	el	em**bra**gue	ehm-**brah**-gheh
clutch assembly	el	con**jun**to de em**bra**gue	kohn-**hoon**-toh deh ehm-**brah**-gheh
pressure plate	el	**pla**to o**pre**sor	**plah**-toh oh-preh-**sohr**

© 2000 Kathy Parsons, Spanish for Cruisers

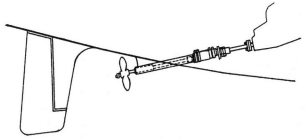

shaft	el	eje	eh-heh
	la	flecha *(Mexico)*	fleh-chah
input shaft	el	eje de entrada	eh-heh deh ehn-trah-dah
	la	flecha de entrada *(Mexico)*	fleh-chah deh ehn-trah-dah
output shaft	el	eje de salida	eh-heh deh sah-lee-dah
	la	flecha de salida *(Mexico)*	fleh-chah deh sah-lee-dah
bearing	el	cojinete	koh-hee-neh-teh
	el	balero	bah-leh-roh
yoke	la	horquilla	ohr-kee-yah
gear shift lever	la	palanca de cambios	pah-lahn-kah deh kahm-byohss
control cable	el	cable de control	kah-bleh deh kohn-trohl
	el	cable de mando	kah-bleh deh mahn-doh

© 2000 Kathy Parsons, Spanish for Cruisers

Transmission Cooling, Lubrication and Fluids			
dipstick	la	va·ri·lla **del** ni·**vel** de a·**cei**·te	vah-**ree**-yah **dehl** nee-**vehl** deh ah-**say**-teh
oil pump	la	**bom**·ba **de** a·**cei**·te	**bohm**-bah **deh** ah-**say**-teh
oil seal	el	**se**·llo **de** a·**cei**·te	**seh**-yoh **deh** ah-**say**-teh
oil cooler	el	en·fria·**dor del** a·**cei**·te	ehn-fryah-**dohr deh** ah-**say**-teh
hydraulic fluid	el	a·**cei**·te hi·**dráu**·li·co	ah-**say**-teh ee-**drow**-lee-koh
transmission fluid	el	a·**cei**·te **de** trans·mi·**sión**	ah-**say**-teh **deh** trahnss-mee-**syohn**

Coupling, Propeller Shaft			
coupling	el	en·**gan**·che	ehn-**gahn**-cheh
	el	a·co·pla·**mien**·to	ah-koh-plah-**myehn**-toh
	el	**co**·ple	**koh**-pleh
flexible coupling	el	en·**gan**·che fle·**xi**·ble	ehn-**gahn**-cheh fleh-**ksee**-bleh
propeller shaft	el	**e**·je **de la hé**·li·ce	**eh**-heh **deh lah eh**-lee-seh
	la	**fle**·cha **de la hé**·li·ce	**fleh**-chah **deh lah eh**-lee-seh
keyway	la	ra·**nu**·ra	rah-**noo**-rah
	la	cha·**ve**·te·ra	chah-veh-**teh**-rah
key	la	**lla**·ve	**yah**-veh
	la	cha·**ve**·ta	chah-**veh**-tah
set screw	el	tor·**ni**·llo **sin** ca·**be**·za	tohr-**nee**-yoh **seen** kah-**beh**-sah
engine mount	el	so·**por**·te **del** mo·**tor**	soh-**pohr**-teh **dehl** moh-**tohr**
alignment	la	a·li·ne·a·**ción**	ah-lee-neh-ah-**syohn**

© 2000 Kathy Parsons, Spanish for Cruisers

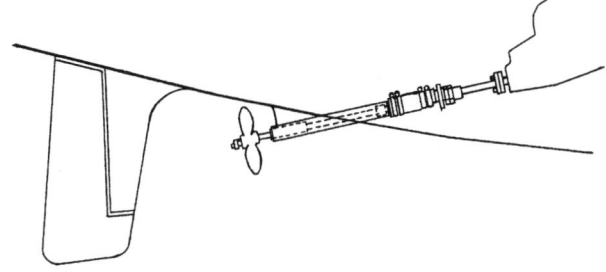 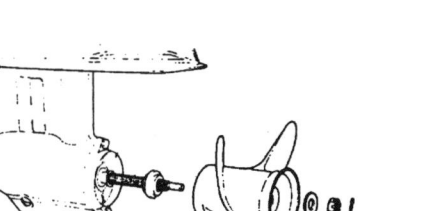

stuffing box	la	pren·sa·es·**to**·pas	prehn-sah-ehss-**toh**-pahss
	el	es·to·**pe**·ro	ehss-toh-**peh**-roh
packing	la	em·pa·que·ta·**du**·ra	ehm-pah-keh-tah-**doo**-rah
	el	em·**pa**·que	ehm-**pah**-keh
stern tube	la	bo·**ci**·na	boh-**see**-nah
cutlass bearing	el	**bu**·je	**boo**-heh
propeller	la	**hé**·li·ce	**eh**-lee-seh
	la	pro·**pe**·la	proh-**peh**-lah
blade	la	**pa**·la	**pah**-lah
3-bladed propeller	la	**hé**·li·ce **de tres pa**·las	eh-lee-seh **deh trehss** pah-lahss
pitch	el	**pa**·so	**pah**-soh
fixed pitch	el	**pa**·so **fi**·jo	**pah**-soh **fee**-hoh
variable pitch	el	**pa**·so va·**ria**·ble	**pah**-soh vah-**ryah**-bleh

© 2000 Kathy Parsons, Spanish for Cruisers

English	article	Spanish	pronunciation
left-handed (turning)		**de gi**ro **a la** iz**quier**da	**deh** hee-roh ah lah eess-**kyehr**-dah
right-handed (turning)		**de gi**ro **a la** de**re**cha	**deh** hee-roh ah lah deh-**reh**-chah
strut (of shaft)	el el	so**por**te arbo**tan**te	soh-**pohr**-teh ahr-boh-**tahn**-teh
propeller nut	la	**tuer**ca **de la hé**li·ce	**twehr**-kah deh lah eh-lee-seh
zinc anode	el	**á**no·do **de zinc**	ah-noh-doh **deh seenk**
cotter pin	la el	cha·**ve**ta pa·sa·**dor**	chah-**veh**-tah pah-sah-**dohr**
Can you ...?		¿**Pue**de ...?	Pweh-deh ...?
... tighten the stuffing box		... a·pre**tar la** pren·sa·es**to**pas ... a·pre**tar el** es·to·**pe**ro *(Mexico)*	ah-preh-**tahr** lah prehn-sah-ehss-**toh**-pahss ah-preh-**tahr ehl** ehss-toh-**peh**-roh
... straighten the propeller shaft **		... en·de·re**zar el** e·je **de la hé**li·ce	ehn-deh-reh-**sahr ehl** eh-heh **deh lah** eh-lee-seh
The propeller is damaged.		**La hé**li·ce es·**tá** da·**ña**·da. **La** pro·**pe**la es·**tá** da·**ña**·da.	**Lah** eh-lee-seh ehss-**tah** dah-**nyah**-dah. **Lah** proh-**peh**-lah ehss-**tah** dah-**nyah**-dah.
The propeller shaft is bent. **		**El** e·je **de la hé**li·ce es·**tá** do·**bla**·do.	**Ehl** eh-heh **deh lah** eh-lee-seh ehss-**tah** doh-**blah**-doh.
It pulls to the left in reverse.		**Se ja**·la **a la** iz**quier**da **en** re·**ver**sa.	**Seh hah**-lah **ah lah** ees-**kyehr**-dah **ehn** reh-**vehr**-sah.

** *In Mexico use **la flecha** in place of **el eje** for **the shaft***

© 2000 Kathy Parsons, Spanish for Cruisers

steering	el	go·**bier**·no	goh-**byehr**-noh
	el	ma·**ne**·jo	mah-**neh**-hoh
	la	di·rec·**ción**	dee-rehk-**syohn**
helm, rudder	el	ti·**món**	tee-**mohn**
tiller	la	**ca**·ña **del** ti·**món**	**kah**-nyah **dehl** tee-**mohn**
steering wheel	el	ti·**món**	tee-**mohn**
	la	**rue**·da	**rweh**-dah
	el	vo·**lan**·te *(Mexico)*	voh-**lahn**-teh
hydraulic steering	el	go·**bier**·no hi·**dráu**·li·co	goh-**byehr**-noh ee-drow-lee-koh
manual steering	el	go·**bier**·no ma·**nual**	goh-**byehr**-noh mah-**nwahl**
reservoir	el	de·**pó**·si·to	deh-**poh**-see-toh

© 2000 Kathy Parsons, Spanish for Cruisers

cylinder	el	ci·lin·dro	see-**leen**-droh
pump	la	**bom**·ba	**bohm**-bah
hydraulic lines	la	tu·be·**rí·a** hi·**dráu**·li·ca	too-beh-**ree**-ah ee-**drow**-lee-kah
hydraulic ram, piston	el	pis·**tón** hi·**dráu**·li·co	peess-**tohn** ee-**drow**-lee-koh
hydraulic fluid	el	a·**cei**·te hi·**dráu**·li·co	ah-**say**-teh ee-**drow**-lee-koh
valve assembly	el	con·**jun**·to **de vál**·vu·las	kohn-**hoon**-toh **deh vahl**-voo-lahss
rack and pinion	la	cre·ma·**lle**·ra **y** pi·**ñon**	kreh-mah-**yeh**-rah **ee** peen-yon
quadrant	el	sec·**tor**	sehk-**tohr**
steering cable	el	**ca**·ble **de** go·**bier**·no	**kah**-bleh **deh** goh-**byehr**-noh
steering chain	la	ca·**de**·na **de** go·**bier**·no	kah-**deh**-nah **deh** goh-**byehr**-noh
worm gear	el	tor·**ni**·llo sin·**fín**	tohr-**nee**-yoh seen-**feen**
pintle	el	**ma**·cho **del** ti·**món**	**mah**-choh **dehl** tee-**mohn**
gudgeon	la	**hem**·bra **del** ti·**món**	**ehm**-brah **dehl** tee-**mohn**
belt	la	co·**rre**·a	koh-**rreh**-ah
	la	**ban**·da *(Mexico)*	**bahn**-dah
autopilot	el	pi·**lo**·to au·to·**má**·ti·co	pee-**loh**-toh ow-toh-**mah**-tee-koh

© 2000 Kathy Parsons, Spanish for Cruisers

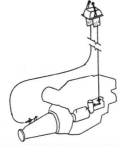

controls	los	**man**·dos	**mahn**-dohss
	los	con**tro**·les	kohn-**troh**-lehss
start button	el	bo**tón de a·rran**que	boh-**tohn deh** ah-**rrahn**-keh
glow plug	la	bu**jí**a **de** pre·ca·len·ta·**mien**·to	boo-**hee**-ah **deh** preh-kah-lehn-tah-**myehn**-toh
starting handle	la	pa·**lan**·ca **de a·rran**·que	pah-**lahn**-kah **deh** ah-**rrahn**-keh
decompression lever	el	des·com·pre·**sor**	deh-kohm-preh-**sohr**
accelerator, throttle	el	a·ce·le·ra·**dor**	ah-seh-leh-rah-**dohr**
lever	la	pa·**lan**·ca	pah-**lahn**-kah
control cable	el	**ca**·ble **de** con·**trol**	**kah**-bleh **deh** kohn-**trohl**
	el	**ca**·ble **de man**·do	**kah**-bleh **deh mahn**-doh
control cable *(Morse type)*	el	**ca**·ble **ti**·po **Mor**·se	**kah**-bleh **tee**-poh **mohr**-seh
instruments	los	in·stru·**men**·tos	een-stroo-**mehn**-tohss
alarm	la	a·**lar**·ma	ah-**lahr**-mah
ammeter	el	am·pe·**rí**·me·tro	ahm-peh-**ree**-meh-troh

© 2000 Kathy Parsons, Spanish for Cruisers

battery charge indicator	el	in·di·ca·**dor de car**·ga **de** ba·te·**rí**a	een-dee-kah-**dohr** deh **kahr**-gah **deh** bah-teh-**ree**-ah
fuel gauge	el	in·di·ca·**dor de** com·bus·ti·ble	een-dee-kah-**dohr deh** kohm-booss-**tee**-bleh
gauge	el	in·di·ca·**dor**	een-dee-kah-**dohr**
	el	me·di·**dor**	meh-dee-**dohr**
	el	mar·ca·**dor**	mahr-kah-**dohr**
	el	re·**loj** *(also means clock)*	reh-**loh**
gauge, pressure	el	ma·**nó**·me·tro	mah-**noh**-meh-troh
oil pressure gauge	el	in·di·ca·**dor de la** pre·**sión del** a·**cei**·te	een-dee-kah-**dohr** deh **lah** preh-**syohn dehl** ah-**say**-teh
tachometer	el	ta·**có**·me·tro	tah-**koh**-meh-troh
temperature gauge	el	ter·**mó**·me·tro	tehr-**moh**-meh-troh
vacuum gauge	el	in·di·ca·**dor de** va·**cí**o	een-dee-kah-**dohr** deh vah-**see**-oh
voltmeter	el	vol·**tí**·me·tro	vohl-**tee**-meh-troh

Instrument Readings

RPM		**RPM**	eh-reh peh eh-meh
oil pressure	la	pre·**sión del** a·**cei**·te	preh-**syohn dehl** ah-**say**-teh
PSI		**PSI**	peh eh-seh ee
water temperature	la	tem·pe·ra·**tu**·ra **del** a·gua	tehm-peh-rah-**too**-rah **dehl** ah-gwah
degrees *(temperature, etc.)*	los	**gra**·dos	**grah**-dohss
volts	los	**vol**·tios	**vohl**-tyohss
amps	los	am·**pe**·rios	ahm-**peh**-ryohss
needle	la	a·**gu**·ja	ah-**goo**-hah

© 2000 Kathy Parsons, Spanish for Cruisers

starter motor	el	mo·tor de a·rran·que	moh-**tohr** deh ah-**rrahn**-keh
armature	la	arma·**du**·ra	ahr-mah-**doo**-rah
battery cable terminal	el	termi·**nal a la** ba·te·**rí**a	tehr-mee-**nahl** **ah** **lah** bah-teh-**ree**-ah
brush (carbon)	el	car**bón**	kahr-**bohn**
	la	es·co·**bi**·lla (**de** car**bón**)	ehss-koh-**bee**-yah (**deh** kahr-**bohn**)
bushing	el	**bu**·je	**boo**-heh
	el	cas·**qui**·llo	kahss-**kee**-yoh
clutch	el	em·**bra**·gue	ehm-**brah**-gheh
commutator	el	con·mu·ta·**dor**	kohn-moo-tah-**dohr**
cover	la	**ta**·pa	**tah**-pah
drive gear (pinion)	el	pi·**ñón** im·pul·**sor**	pe-**nyohn** eem-pool-**sohr**
field coils	las	bo·**bi**·nas **de cam**·po	boh-**bee**-nahss **deh kahm**-poh
fork, yoke	la	hor·**qui**·lla	ohr-**kee**-yah
housing	la	car·**ca**·sa	kahr-**kah**-sah
ignition switch terminal	el	termi·**nal a la lla**·ve	tehr-mee-**nahl** **ah** **lah** **yah**-veh

© 2000 Kathy Parsons, Spanish for Cruisers

link	el	es·la·**bón**	ehss-lah-**bohn**
relay	el	re·**lé**	reh-**leh** (*also* **ree**-leh)
winding	el	em·bo·bi·**na**·do	ehm-boh-bee-**nah**-doh
solenoid	el	so·le·**noi**·de	soh-leh-**noy**-deh
	el	au·to·**má**·tico	ow-toh-**mah**-tee-koh
electromagnet	el	e·lec·tro·i·**mán**	eh-lehk-troh-ee-**mahn**
coil	la	bo·**bi**·na	boh-**bee**-nah
points	los	con·**tac**·tos	kohn-**tahk**-tohss
	los	pla·**ti**·nos	plah-**tee**-yohss
ground	la	**tie**·rra	**tyeh**-rrah
spring	el	re·**sor**·te	reh-**sohr**-teh
cover	la	**ta**·pa	**tah**-pah
plunger	el	**ém**·bo·lo	**ehm**-boh-loh
	el	pis·**tón**	pees-**tohn**
The engine doesn't start.	**El** mo·**tor** **no** a·**rran**·ca. **El** mo·**tor** **no** **pren**·de.		**Ehl** moh-**tohr** noh ah-**rrahn**-kah. **Ehl** moh-**tohr** noh **prehn**-deh.
It is difficult to start the motor.	**Es** di·**fí**·cil a·rran·**car** **el** mo·**tor**.		**Ehss** dee-fee-seel ah-rrahn-**kahr** ehl moh-**tohr**.
The engine doesn't turn over (crank).	**El** mo·**tor** **no** **gi**·ra.		**Ehl** moh-**tohr** noh **hee**-rah.
The engine turns over very slowly.	**El** mo·**tor** **gi**·ra **muy** des·**pa**·cio.		**Ehl** moh-**tohr** **hee**-rah **mwee** dehss-**pah**-syoh.

© 2000 Kathy Parsons, Spanish for Cruisers

alternator	el	alterna**dor**	ahl-tehr-nah-**dohr**
bearing	el	coji**ne**te	koh-hee-**neh**-teh
	el	ba**le**ro *(Mexico)*	bah-**leh**-roh
belt	la	co**rre**a	koh-**rreh**-ah
	la	**ban**da *(Mexico)*	**bahn**-dah
brush	el	car**bón**	kahr-**bohn**
	la	esco**bi**lla	ehss-koh-**bee**-yah
capacitor, condenser	el	conden·sa**dor**	kohn-dehn-sah-**dohr**
diode	el	**dio**do	**dyoh**-doh
fan	el	venti·la**dor**	vehn-tee-lah-**dohr**
field terminal	el	termi·**nal de cam**po	tehr-mee-**nahl deh kahm**-poh
field windings	el	embo·bi**na**do **de cam**po	ehm-boh-bee-**nah**-doh **deh kahm**-poh
housing	la	car**ca**sa	kahr-**kah**-sah
isolation diode	el	**dio**do ais**lan**te	**dyoh**-doh eyess-**lahn**-teh
pulley	la	po**le**a	poh-**leh**-ah
rectifier	el	rectifi·ca**dor**	rehk-tee-fee-kah-**dohr**

© 2000 Kathy Parsons, Spanish for Cruisers

retainer	el	re·te·ne·**dor**	reh-teh-neh-**dohr**
rotor	el	ro·**tor**	roh-**tohr**
rotor windings	el	em·bo·bi·**na**·do **del** ro·**tor**	ehm-boh-bee-**nah**-doh **dehl** roh-**tohr**
slip rings	los	a·**ni**·llos des·li·**za**·bles	ah-**nee**-yohss dehss-lee-**sah**-blehss
stator	el	es·ta·**tor**	ehss-tah-**tohr**
regulator (voltage)	el	re·gu·la·**dor** (**de** vol·ta·je)	reh-goo-lah-**dohr** (**deh** vohl-**tah**-heh)
charge indicator	el	in·di·ca·**dor** de **car**·ga	een-dee-kah-**dohr** deh **kahr**-gah
diode	el	**dio**·do	**dyoh**-doh
voltage adjustment	el	a·**jus**·te **de** vol·ta·je	ah-**hooss**-teh **deh** vohl-**tah**-heh
voltage limiter	el	li·mi·ta·**dor** **del** vol·ta·je	lee-mee-tah-**dohr** **dehl** vohl-**tah**-heh
resistor	el la	re·sis·**tor** re·sis·**ten**·cia	reh-seess-**tohr** reh-seess-**tehn**-syah
battery	la el	ba·te·**ría** a·cu·mu·la·**dor**	bah-teh-**ree**-ah ah-koo-moo-lah-**dohr**
battery terminal	el	ter·mi·**nal**	tehr-mee-**nahl**
positive		...po·si·**ti**·vo	poh-see-**tee**-voh
negative		...ne·ga·**ti**·vo	neh-gah-**tee**-voh
battery switch	el el	**switch** **de** ba·te·**ría** des·co·nec·ta·**dor** **de** ba·te·**ría**	ehss-**weetch** **deh** bah-teh-**ree**-ah dehss-koh-nehk-tah-**dohr** **deh** bah-teh-**ree**-ah
3-position ...		... **de** tres po·si·**cio**·nes	... **deh** trehss poh-see-**syoh**-nehss

© 2000 Kathy Parsons, Spanish for Cruisers

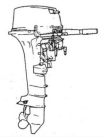

outboard motor	el	mo·**tor** **fue**·ra **de** **bor**·da	moh-**tohr** **fweh**-rah **deh** **bohr**-dah
	el	fue·ra·**bor**·da	fweh-rah-**bohr**-dah
steering arm	el	**bra**·zo **de** di·rec·**ción**	**brah**-soh **deh** dee-rehk-**syohn**
choke	el	es·tran·gu·la·**dor**	ehss-trahn-goo-lah-**dohr**
	el	a·ho·ga·**dor**	ah-oh-gah-**dohr**
	el	**star**·ter	ess-**tahr**-tehr
throttle control lever	la	pa·**lan**·ca **de** con·**trol de** a·ce·le·ra·**ción**	pah-**lahn**-kah **deh** kohn-**trohl deh** ahk-seh-leh-rah-**syohn**
stop button (kill switch)	el	bo·**tón de** a·pa·**gar**	boh-**tohn deh** ah-pah-**gahr**
	el	a·pa·ga·**dor**	ah-pah-gah-**dohr**
idle speed adjustment	el	a·**jus**·te **de mar**·cha **en ba**·ja	ah-**hoos**-teh **deh mahr**-chah **ehn bah**-hah
engine cover	la	**ta**·pa **del** mo·**tor**	**tah**-pah **deh** moh-**tohr**
shift lever	la	pa·**lan**·ca **de cam**·bios	pah-**lahn**-kah **deh kahm**-byohss
linkage	la	ar·ti·cu·la·**ción**	ahr-tee-koo-lah-**syohn**
starter cord	la	**cuer**·da **de** a·**rran**·que	**kwehr**-dah **deh** ah-**rrahn**-keh

© 2000 Kathy Parsons, Spanish for Cruisers

English	Article	Spanish	Pronunciation
stern brackets	los	soportes de popa	soh-**pohr**-tehss **deh poh**-pah
clamp screws	los	tornillos de sujección	tohr-**nee**-yohss **deh** soo-hehk-**syohn**
tilt friction nut	la	tuerca de fricción de inclinación	**twehr**-kah **deh** freek-**syohn deh** een-klee-nah-**syohn**
angle adjusting rod	la	varilla del ajuste del ángulo	vah-**ree**-yah **dehl** ah-**hoos**-teh **dehl** ahn-goo-loh
tilt support	el	soporte de inclinación	soh-**pohr**-teh **deh** een-klee-nah-**syohn**
tilt	la	inclinación	een-klee-nah-**syohn**
fuel	el	combustible	kohm-booss-**tee**-bleh
gasoline	la	gasolina *(not "gas"!)*	gah-soh-**lee**-nah
mixture	la	mezcla	**mehss**-klah
100:1		**cien a uno**	**syehn a oo**-noh
50:1		cincuenta a uno	seen-**kwehn**-tah **ah oo**-noh
break-in period	el	**tiempo de** aflojar el motor	**tyehm**-poh **deh** ah-floh-**hahr ehl** moh-**tohr**
	el	asientamiento del motor	ah-syehn-tah-**myehn**-toh **dehl** moh-**tohr**
fuel hose	la	manguera de combustible	mahn-**gheh**-rah **deh** kohm-booss-**tee**-bleh
fuel connector	el	conector de combustible	koh-nehk-**tohr deh** kohm-booss-**tee**-bleh
primer bulb	la	bombita de ceba	bohm-**bee**-tah **deh seh**-bah
tank	el	**tanque**	**tahn**-keh
filler cap	el	tapón	tah-**pohn**
vent screw	el	tornillo de ventilación	tohr-**nee**-yoh **deh** vehn-tee-lah-**syohn**

© 2000 Kathy Parsons, Spanish for Cruisers

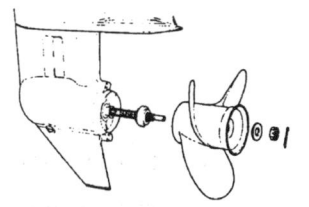

lower unit	la	**co**·la	**koh**-lah
skeg, keel	la	**qui**·lla	**kee**-yah
anti-cavitation plate	el	**pla**·to **an**·ti-ca·vita·**ción**	**plah**-toh **ahn**-tee-kah-vee-tah-**syohn**
water intake	la	**to**·ma **de a**·gua	**toh**-mah **deh ah**-gwah
water pump	la	**bom**·ba **de a**·gua	**bohm**-bah **deh ah**-gwah
exhaust water discharge	la	des·**car**·ga **de a**·gua **de** es·**ca**·pe	dehss-**kahr**-gah **deh ah**-gwah **deh** ehss-**kah**-peh
exhaust relief	el	a·**li**·vio **de** es·**ca**·pe	ah-**lee**-vyoh **deh** ehss-**kah**-peh
gear case	la	**ca**·ja **de** en·**gra**·nes	**kah**-hah **deh** ehn-**grah**-nehss
	la	**ca**·ja **de cam**·bios	**kah**-hah **deh kahm**-byohss
oil level plug	el	ta·**pón de** ni·**vel de** a·**cei**·te	tah-**pohn deh** nee-**vehl deh** ah-**say**-teh
oil drain plug	el	ta·**pón de** dre·**na**·je	tah-**pohn deh** dreh-**nah**-heh
oil fill plug	el	ta·**pón de** lle·**na**·do **de** a·**cei**·te	tah-**pohn deh** yeh-**nah**-doh **deh** ah-**say**-teh
zinc anode	el	**á**·no·do **de zinc**	**ah**-noh-doh de **seenk**

© 2000 Kathy Parsons, Spanish for Cruisers

propeller	la	**hé**·li·ce	**eh**-lee-seh
	la	pro·**pe**·la	proh-**peh**-lah
blade	la	**pa**·la	**pah**-lah
pitch	el	**pa**·so **de la hé**·li·ce	**pah**-soh **deh lah eh**-lee-seh
cotter pin	la	cha·**ve**·ta	chah-**veh**-tah
	el	pa·sa·**dor**	pah-sah-**dohr**
drive pin	el	pa·sa·**dor de** pro·pul·**sión**	pah-sah-**dohr deh** proh-pool-**syohn**
propeller shaft	el	**e**·je **de la hé**·li·ce	**eh**-heh **deh lah eh**-lee-seh
	la	**fle**·cha **de la hé**·li·ce *(Mexico)*	fleh-chah **deh lah eh**-lee-seh

| It was submerged ... | **Se** hun·**dió ...** | **Seh** oon-**dyoh ...** |
| ... in salt water. | ... **en a**·gua sa·**la**·da. | ... **ehn** ah-gwah sah-**lah**-dah. |

| It doesn't plane any more ... | **Ya no** pla·**ne**·a ... | **Yah noh** plah-**neh**-ah ... |
| ... with 2 people. | ... **con dos** per·**so**·nas. | ... **kohn dohss** pehr-**soh**-nahss. |

| The propeller is damaged. | **La hé**·li·ce es·**tá** da·**ña**·da. | **Lah eh**-lee-seh ehss-**tah** dah-**nyah**-dah. |
| | **La** pro·**pe**·la es·**tá** da·**ña**·da. | **Lah** proh-**peh**-lah ehss-**tah** dah-**nyah**-dah. |

| No exhaust water comes out. | **No sa**·le **a**·gua **del** es·**ca**·pe. | **Noh sah**-leh ah-gwah **dehl** ehss-**kah**-peh. |

© 2000 Kathy Parsons, Spanish for Cruisers

Use these SENTENCE STARTERS with the ACTION PHRASES below.		
I need (to) ...	Ne·ce·si·to ...	Neh-seh-**see**-toh ...
Do I need (to) ...?	¿Ne·ce·si·to ...?	Neh-seh-**see**-toh ...?
I am going to ...	**Voy a** ...	**Voy ah** ...
Can you ...?	¿**Pue**·de ...?	**Pweh**-deh ...?
I can't ...	**No pue**·do ...	**Noh pweh**-doh ...

Start, stop the engine

start the engine	a·rran·**car el mo**·**tor**	ah-rrahn-**kahr ehl** moh-**tohr**
	pren·**der el mo**·tor	prehn-**dehr ehl** moh-**tohr**
	en·cen·**der el mo**·tor	ehn-sehn-**dehr ehl** moh-**tohr**
turn off the engine	a·pa·**gar el mo**·tor	ah-pah-**gahr ehl** moh-**tohr**
stop the engine	pa·**rar el mo**·tor	pah-**rahr ehl** moh-**tohr**
crank the engine	**dar** a·**rran**·que **al mo**·tor	**dahr** ah-rrahn-keh **ahl** moh-**tohr**
prime the engine	ce·**bar el mo**·tor	seh-**bahr ehl** moh-**tohr**

Throttle and Speed

idle	o·pe·**rar a ba**·ja re·vo·lu·**ción**	oh-peh-**rahr ah bah**-hah reh-voh-loo-**syohn**
reduce throttle	re·du·**cir la** a·ce·le·ra·**ción**	reh-doo-**seer lah** ah-seh-leh-rah-**syohn**
increase throttle	au·men·**tar la** a·ce·le·ra·**ción**	ow-mehn-**tahr lah** ah-seh-leh-rah-**syohn**
increase speed	au·men·**tar la** ve·lo·ci·**dad**	ow-mehn-**tahr lah** veh-loh-see-**dahd**
reduce speed	re·du·**cir la** ve·lo·ci·**dad**	reh-doo-**seer lah** veh-loh-see-**dahd**
plane	pla·ne·**ar**	plah-neh-**ahr**

© 2000 Kathy Parsons, Spanish for Cruisers

Put in gear		
put in gear	po·**ner en mar**·cha	poh-**nehr ehn mahr**-chah
put in forward gear	po·**ner en mar**·cha a·de·**lan**·te	poh-**nehr ehn mahr**-chah ah-deh-**lahn**-teh
put in reverse gear	po·**ner en** re·**ver**·sa	poh-**nehr ehn** reh-**vehr**-sah
put in neutral	po·**ner en** neu·**tral**	poh-**nehr ehn** neh-oo-**trahl**
engage (the clutch)	em·bra·**gar**	ehm-brah-**gahr**

Turn left, right		
turn left	do·**blar a la** iz·**quier**·da	doh-**blahr ah lah** eess-**kyehr**-dah
turn right	do·**blar a la** de·**re**·cha	doh-**blahr ah lah** deh-**reh**-chah

Turn to port, starboard		
turn to port	do·**blar al** ba·**bor**	doh-**blahr ahl** bah-**bohr**
turn to starboard	do·**blar al** es·tri·**bor**	doh-**blahr ahl** ehss-tree-**bohr**

a little (more)	**un po**·co (**más**)	**oon poh**-koh **mahss**
more!	**¡más!**	**mahss!**
Enough!, Now!	**¡Ya!**	**Yah!**
	¡Bas·ta!	**Bahss**-tah!

slow	des·**pa**·cio	dehss-**pah**-syoh
	len·to	**lehn**-toh
fast	**rá**·pi·do	**rah**-pee-doh

↑ a·de·**lan**·te *(forward)*

← **a la** iz·**quier**·da *(to the left)*   ~ neu·**tral** *(neutral)*   *(to the right)* **a la** de·**re**·cha →
← **al** ba·**bor** *(to port)*   *(to starboard)* **al** es·tri·**bor** →

↓ re·**ver**·sa *(reverse)*
↓ a·**trás** *(back, backwards)*

© 2000 Kathy Parsons, Spanish for Cruisers

To talk about what you need to have done on your boat, add an ACTION PHRASE to the SENTENCE and QUESTIONS STARTERS below. Examples:

I need to + fill the tank.	Necesito + llenar el tanque.
Can you + check the alternator?	¿Puede + revisar el alternador?
How much does it cost to + fix the outboard?	¿Cuánto cuesta + reparar el fueraborda?
Do I need to + pull the motor?	¿Necesito + sacar el motor?

Sentence starters

I need (to) ...	Necesito ...	Neh-seh-see-toh ...
I want (to) ...	Quiero	Kyeh-roh ...
I am going to ...	Voy a ...	Voy ah ...
I can ...	Puedo ...	Pweh-doh ...
I can't ...	No puedo ...	Noh pweh-doh ...

Question starters

Do I need (to) ...?	¿Necesito ...?	Neh-seh-see-toh ...?
Can you ...?	¿Puede ...?	Pweh-deh ...?
Are you going to ...?	¿Va a ...?	Vah ah ...?
How much does it cost (to) ...?	¿Cuánto cuesta ...?	Kwahn-toh kwehss-tah ....?
How much time do you need to ..?	¿Cuánto tiempo necesita para ...?	Kwahn-toh tyehm-poh neh-seh-see-tah pah-rah ...?

© 2000 Kathy Parsons, Spanish for Cruisers

add (liquid), pour	echar	eh-**chahr**
add oil	echar aceite	eh-**chahr** ah-**say**-teh
adjust	ajustar	ah-hooss-**tahr**
adjust the belt	ajustar la correa (**ban**da –*Mexico*)	ah-hoos-**tahr** lah koh-**rreh**-ah (**bahn**-dah)
align the engine	alinear el motor	ah-lee-neh-**ahr** ehl moh-**tohr**
bolt on	atornillar	ah-tohr-nee-**yahr**
change, replace	cambiar	kahm-**byahr**
replace the impeller	cambiar el impulsor	kahm-**byahr** ehl eem-pool-**sohr**
change the oil and filter	cambiar el aceite y el filtro	kahm-**byahr** ehl ah-**say**-teh ee ehl **feel**-troh
charge the battery	cargar la batería	kahr-**gahr** lah bah-teh-**ree**-ah
check, inspect	revisar	reh-vee-sahr
check the oil level	revisar el nivel de aceite	reh-vee-**sahr** ehl nee-**vehl** deh ah-**say**-teh
check the propeller shaft zinc	revisar el ánodo **del** eje **de la** hélice	reh-vee-**sahr** ehl ah-**noh**-doh **dehl** **eh**-heh **deh** lah **eh**-lee-seh
clean	limpiar	leem-**pyahr**
clean the connections	limpiar las conexiones	leem-**pyahr** lahss koh-neh-**ksyoh**-nehss
clean the carburetor	limpiar el carburador	leem-**pyahr** ehl kahr-boo-rah-**dohr**

© 2000 Kathy Parsons, Spanish for Cruisers

Sentence starters

I need (to) ...	Necesito ...	Neh-seh-**see**-toh ...
I want (to) ...	**Quie**ro	**Kyeh**-roh ...
I am going to ...	**Voy a** ...	**Voy ah** ...
I can ...	**Pue**do ...	**Pweh**-doh ...
I can't ...	**No pue**do ...	**Noh pweh**-doh ...

Question starters

Do I need to ...?	¿Necesito ...?	Neh-seh-**see**-toh ...?
Can you ...?	¿**Pue**de ...?	**Pweh**-deh ...?
Are you going to ...?	¿**Va a** ...?	**Vah ah** ...?
How much does it cost (to) ...?	¿**Cuán**to **cues**ta ...?	**Kwahn**-toh **kwehss**-tah ....?
How much time do you need to ..?	¿**Cuán**to **tiem**po necesita **pa**ra ...?	**Kwahn**-toh **tyehm**-poh neh-seh-**see**-tah **pah**-rah ...?

Add one of the following ACTION PHRASES *to the* SENTENCE *or* QUESTION STARTERS *from above:*

connect	conec**tar**	koh-nehk-**tahr**
connect the fuel hose	conec**tar la** man**gue**ra **de** combus**ti**ble	koh-nehk-**tahr lah** mahn-**gheh**-rah **deh** kohm-boohss-**tee**-bleh
cut	cor**tar**	kohr-**tahr**
decarbonize the exhaust	descarboni**zar el** es**ca**pe	dehss-kahr-boh-nee-**sahr ehl** ehss-kah-peh
disconnect	desconec**tar**	dehss-koh-nehk-**tahr**

© 2000 Kathy Parsons, Spanish for Cruisers

drain the oil	vaciar el aceite	vah-**syahr** ehl ah-**say**-teh
drill	ta·la·**drar**	tah-lah-**drahr**
fill the tank	lle·**nar el tan**·que	yeh-**nahr ehl tahn**-keh
finish	ter·mi·**nar**	tehr-mee-**nahr**
fix, repair	re·pa·**rar** a·rre·**glar**	reh-pah-**rahr** ah-rreh-**glahr**
grease	en·gra·**sar**	ehn-grah-**sahr**
grind	es·me·ri·**lar**	ehss-meh-ree-**lahr**
loosen the bolt, screw	a·flo·**jar el** tor·**ni**·llo	ah-floh-**hahr ehl** tohr-**nee**-yoh
lubricate	lu·bri·**car**	loo-bree-**kahr**
measure	me·**dir**	meh-**deer**
measure the compression	me·**dir la** com·pre·**sión**	meh-**deer lah** kohm-preh-**syohn**
measure the voltage	me·**dir el** vol·**ta**·je	meh-**deer ehl** vohl-**tah**-heh
overhaul	re·con·**struir**	reh-kohn-stroo-**eer**
overhaul the injectors	re·con·**struir los** in·yec·**to**·res	reh-kohn-stroo-**eer lohss** een-yehk-**toh**-rehss
paint	pin·**tar**	peen-**tahr**
polish	pu·**lir**	poo-**leer**
pressure-wash	lim·**piar a** pre·**sión**	leem-**pyahr ah** preh-**syohn**
pull the engine	sa·**car el** mo·**tor**	sah-**kahr ehl** moh-**tohr**
purge the air from ...	sa·**car** ai·re de ...	sah-**kahr eye**-reh deh ...

© 2000 Kathy Parsons, Spanish for Cruisers

Sentence starters

I need (to) ...	Ne·ce·**si**·to ...	Neh-seh-**see**-toh ...
I want (to) ...	**Quie**ro	**Kyeh**-roh ...
I am going to ...	**Voy a** ...	Voy ah ...
I can ...	**Pue**do ...	**Pweh**-doh ...
I can't ...	**No pue**do ...	Noh **pweh**-doh ...

Question starters

Do I need (to) ...?	¿Ne·ce·**si**·to ...?	Neh-seh-**see**-toh ...?
Can you ...?	¿**Pue**de ...?	**Pweh**-deh ...?
Are you going to ...?	¿**Va a** ...?	Vah ah ...?
How much does it cost (to) ...?	¿**Cuán**·to **cues**·ta ...?	**Kwahn**-toh **kwehss**-tah ....?
How much time do you need to..?	¿**Cuán**·to **tiem**·po ne·ce·**si**·ta **pa**·ra ...?	**Kwahn**-toh **tyehm**-poh neh-seh-**see**-tah **pah**-rah..?

Add one of the following phrases to the Sentence or Question Starters from above:

raise the engine	le·van·**tar el** mo·**tor**	leh-vahn-**tahr ehl** moh-**tohr**
reline the cylinders *(change the liners)*	cam·**biar las** ca·**mi**·sas **de** ci·**lin**·dro	kahm-**byahr lahss** kah-**mee**-sahss **deh** see-**leen**-droh
remove, haul out	sa·**car** qui·**tar** *(remove, but not haul)*	sah-**kahr** kee-**tahr**

© 2000 Kathy Parsons, Spanish for Cruisers

sand	li·**jar**	lee-**hahr**
scrape	ras·**par**	rahss-**pahr**
solder the connection	sol·**dar** la co·nec·**ción**	sohl-**dahr** lah koh-nehk-**syohn**
straighten the propeller	en·de·re·**zar** la **hé**·li·ce	ehn-deh-reh-**sahr** lah **eh**-lee-seh
switch off	des·co·nec·**tar**	dehss-koh-nehk-**tahr**
test	pro·**bar**	proh-**bahr**
test the thermostat	pro·**bar** **el** ter·mos·**ta**·to	proh-**bahr** ehl tehr-mohss-**tah**-toh
tighten	a·pre·**tar**	ah-preh-**tahr**
tighten the bolt, screw	a·pre·**tar** **el** tor·**ni**·llo	ah-preh-**tahr** ehl tohr-**nee**-yoh
tune up the engine	a·fi·**nar** **el** mo·**tor**	ah-fee-**nahr** ehl moh-**tohr**
turn	gi·**rar**	hee-**rahr**
turn to the right / clockwise	gi·**rar** **a** **la** de·**re**·cha	hee-**rahr** ah lah deh-**reh**-chah
turn to the left / counter-clockwise	gi·**rar** **a** **la** iz·**quier**·da	hee-**rahr** ah lah eess-**kyehr**-dah
turn on, off		
turn off	a·pa·**gar**	ah-pah-**gahr**
turn on	pren·**der**	prehn-**dehr**
	en·cen·**der**	ehn-sehn-**dehr**
weld	sol·**dar**	sohl-**dahr**
work	tra·ba·**jar**	trah-bah-**hahr**

© 2000 Kathy Parsons, Spanish for Cruisers

16. Working with Engines: Action Phrases (R – Z)

These adjectives are useful for describing almost anything aboard your boat - your equipment, the parts you need, the problems you are having. Here are some ways you might use them:

To describe the current condition of something: *(Be sure you stress the last syllable in es·tá & es·tán!)* **

It is ...	Está .... *(the word "it" is omitted in Spanish.)*	Ehss-**tah** ...
It is broken.	Está roto.	Ehss-tah roh-toh.
The pipe is broken.	El tubo está roto.	Ehl too-boh ehss-tah roh-toh.
They are ...	Están ... *(the word "they" is omitted in Spanish)*	Ehss-tahn ...
They are burnt.	Están quemados.	Ehss-tahn keh-mah-dohss.

To ask about the current condition of something:

Is it ...?	¿Está ....? *(the word "it" is omitted in Spanish)*	Ehss-tah ...?
Is it broken?	¿Está roto?	Ehss-tah roh-toh?
Is it ready?	¿Está listo?	Ehss-tah leess-toh?

To describe what you need: *(you usually place the adjective after the noun)*

Do you have potable water?	¿Tiene agua potable?	Tyeh-neh ah-gwah poh-tah-bleh?
I need a flat washer.	Necesito una arandela plana. (ron·da·na pla·na – Mexico)	Neh-seh-see-toh oo-nah ah-rahr-deh-lah plah-nah. (rohn-dah-nah)

To identify or describe something's permanent characteristics.

It is ...	Es ... *(the word "it" is omitted in Spanish.)*	Ehss ...
It is white.	Es blanco.	Ehss blahn-koh.
The hull is white.	El casco es blanco.	Ehl kahss-koh ehss blahn-koh.

© 2000 Kathy Parsons, Spanish for Cruisers

• •

They are ...	**Son** ... (the word "they" is omitted in Spanish)	**Sohn** ...
They are white.	**Son blan**cos.	**Sohn blahn**-kohss.

** Spanish has 2 different sets of words for **is** and **are**:
es·**tá** and es·**tán** = when describing something's **temporary condition** or **location**
es and **son** = when describing something's **identity** or **permanent characteristics**

But don't sweat it – you will usually be understood whichever you use!

Adjectives

a little	**un po**·co	**oon poh**-koh	broken	**ro**·to	**roh**-toh
a lot	**mu**·cho	**moo**-choh	burnt	que·**ma**·do	keh-**mah**-doh
almost	**ca**·si	**kah**-see	carbonned up	car·boni·**za**·do	kahr-boh-nee-**sah**-doh
attached	**fi**·jo	**fee**-hoh	charged (*battery*)	car·**ga**·do	kahr-**gah**-doh
available	dis·po·**ni**·ble	deess-poh-**nee**-bleh	cheap	ba·**ra**·to	bah-**rah**-toh
bad	**ma**·lo	**mah**-loh	clean	**lim**·pio	**leem**-pyoh
bent	do·**bla**·do	doh-**blah**-doh	closed	ce·**rra**·do	seh-**rrah**-doh
better	me·**jor**	meh-**hohr**	cold	**frí**·o	**free**-oh
big	**gran**·de	**grahn**-deh	connected	co·nec·**ta**·do	koh-nehk-**tah**-doh
black	**ne**·gro	**neh**-groh	correct	co·**rrec**·to	koh-**rrehk**-toh
blocked	blo·que·**a**·do	bloh-keh-**ah**-doh	corroded	co·rro·**í**·do	koh-rroh-**ee**-doh
blown (fuse)	fun·**di**·do	foon-**dee**-doh	cracked	par·**ti**·do	pahr-**tee**-doh
blue	a·**zul**	ah-**sool**	cut	cor·**ta**·do	kohr-**tah**-doh

© 2000 Kathy Parsons, Spanish for Cruisers

It is ... *(current condition)*	Es**tá**	Ehss-**tah** ...
They are ... *(current condition)*	Es**tán** ...	Ehss-**tahn** ...
Is it ...? *(current condition)*	¿Es**tá** ....?	Ehss-**tah** ...?
Do you have ...?	¿**Tie**ne ...?	**Tyeh**-neh ...?
I need	Ne·ce·**si**·to ...	Neh-seh-**see**-toh ...
It is ... *(permanent)*	**Es** ...	Ehss ...
They are ... *(permanent)*	**Son** ...	Sohn ...

Adjectives					
damaged	da·**ña**·do	dah-**nyah**-doh	electric	e·**léc**·tri·co	eh-**lehk**-tree-koh
dangerous	pe·li·**gro**·so	peh-lee-**groh**-soh	empty	va·**cí**·o	vah-**see**-oh
dead *(battery)*	**muer**·to	**mwehr**-toh	enough	su·fi·**cien**·te,	soo-fee-**syehn**-teh
deep	pro·**fun**·do	proh-**foon**-doh		bas·**tan**·te	bahss-**tahn**-teh
difficult	di·**fí**·cil	dee-**fee**-seel	expensive	**ca**·ro	**kah**-roh
direct	di·**rec**·to	dee-**rehk**-toh	external	ex·**ter**·no	ehkss-**tehr**-noh
dirty	**su**·cio	**soo**-syoh	fast	**rá**·pi·do	**rah**-pee-doh
discharged	des·car·**ga**·do	dehss-kahr-**gah**-doh	female *(threads, connectors, etc.)*	**hem**·bra	**ehm**-brah
disconnected	des·co·nec·**ta**·do	dehss-koh-**nehk**-tah-doh	fixed	**fi**·jo	**fee**-hoh
down	a·**ba**·jo	ah-**bah**-hoh	flat	**pla**·no	**plah**-noh
dry	**se**·co	**seh**-koh	flattened	a·plas·**ta**·do,	ah-plahss-**tah**-doh
easy	**fá**·cil	**fah**-seel		a·pla·**na**·do	ah-plah-**nah**-doh

© 2000 Kathy Parsons, Spanish for Cruisers

flooded	a·ho·**ga**·do	ah-oh-**gah**-doh		less	**me**·nos	meh-nohss
foamy *(oil, etc)*	es·pu·**mo**·so	ehss-poo-**moh**-soh		light	li·**ge**·ro	lee-**heh**-roh
forward	a·de·**lan**·te	ah-deh-**lahn**-teh		live	**con** co·**rrien**·te,	**kohn** koh-**ryehn**-teh
fouled	con·ta·mi·**na**·do	kohn-tah-mee-**nah**-doh		*(with current)*	po·si·**ti**·vo	poh-see-**tee**-voh
free *(most uses)*	**li**·bre	**lee**-breh		loaded	car·**ga**·do	kahr-**gah**-doh
free-of-charge	**gra**·tis	**grah**-teess		long	**lar**·go	**lahr**-goh
fresh *(water)*	**dul**·ce	**dool**-seh		loose *(not tight)*	**flo**·jo	**floh**-hoh
full	**lle**·no	**yeh**-noh		loose	**suel**·to	**swehl**-toh
functioning	fun·cio·**nan**·do	foon-syoh-**nahn**-doh		*(unattached)*		
good	**bue**·no	**bweh**-noh		lost	per·**di**·do	pehr-**dee**-doh
ground	**de tie**·rra	**deh tyeh**-rrah		low	**ba**·jo	**bah**-hoh
hand	a·pre·**ta**·do **a**	ah-preh-**tah**-doh **ah**		lower	in·fe·**rior**	een-feh-**ryohr**
tightened	**ma**·no	**mah**-noh		male *(threads,*	**ma**·cho	**mah**-choh
heavy	pe·**sa**·do	peh-**sah**-doh		*connectors, etc.)*		
high	**al**·to	**ahl**-toh		manual	ma·**nual**	mah-**nwahl**
hot	ca·**lien**·te	kah-**lyehn**-teh		many	**mu**·chos	**moo**-chohss
incorrect	in·co·**rrec**·to	een-koh-**rehk**-toh		maximum	**má**·xi·mo	**mah**-ksee-moh
increasing	au·men·**tan**·do	ow-mehn-**tahn**-doh		medium	me·**dia**·no	meh-**dyah**-noh
indirect	in·di·**rec**·to	een-dee-**rehk**-toh		minimum	**mí**·ni·mo	**mee**-nee-moh
insulated	ais·**la**·do	eyess-**lah**-doh		more	**más**	**mahss**
internal	in·**ter**·no	een-**tehr**-noh		much	**mu**·cho	**moo**-choh

© 2000 Kathy Parsons, Spanish for Cruisers

It is ... *(current condition)*	Está	Ehss-**tah** ...
They are ... *(current condition)*	Es**tán** ...	Ehss-**tahn** ...
Is it ...? *(current condition)*	¿Es**tá** ...?	Ehss-**tah** ...?
Do you have ...?	**¿Tie**ne ...?	**Tyeh**-neh ...?
I need	Ne·ce·**si**·to ...	Neh-seh-**see**-toh ...
It is ... *(permanent)*	**Es** ...	Ehss ...
They are ... *(permanent)*	**Son** ...	Sohn ...

Adjectives

negative	ne·ga·**ti**·vo	neh-gah-**tee**-voh	overcharged	so·bre·car·**ga**·do	soh-breh-kahr-**gah**-doh
neutral	**neu**·tro	**noo**-troh	overloaded	so·bre·car·**ga**·do	soh-breh-kahr-**gah**-doh
neutral *(gear)*	neu·**tral**	noo-**trahl**	pitted	pi·**ca**·do	pee-**kah**-doh
new	**nue**·vo	**nweh**-voh	plugged	ta·**pa**·do	tah-**pah**-doh
normal	nor·**mal**	nohr-**mahl**	poor, lean	**po**·bre	**poh**-breh
off *(switch)*	a·pa·**ga**·do	ah-pah-**gah**-doh	positive	po·si·**ti**·vo	poh-see-**tee**-voh
old	**vie**·jo	**vyeh**-hoh	potable *(water)*	po·**ta**·ble	poh-**tah**-bleh
on *(switch)*	pren·**di**·do,	prehn-**dee**-doh	ready	**lis**·to	**leess**-toh
	en·cen·**di**·do	ehn-sehn-**dee**-doh	rebuilt	re·con·**strui**·do	reh-kohn-**strwee**-doh
open	a·**bier**·to	ah-**byehr**-toh	reverse	re·**ver**·sa,	reh-**vehr**-sah
original	o·ri·gi·**nal**	oh-ree-hee-**nahl**		a·**trás**	ah-**trahss**
out of	**fue**·ra de	**fweh**-rah deh	rich	**ri**·co	**ree**-koh
adjustment	a·**jus**·te	ah-**hooss**-teh	rough running	fa·**llan**·do	fah-**yahn**-doh

© 2000 Kathy Parsons, Spanish for Cruisers

round	re**don**do	reh-**dohn**-doh	stuck	pe**ga**do	peh-**gah**-doh
running	fun·cio**nan**do	foon-syoh-**nahn**-doh	tap *(water)*	**del gri**fo,	**dehl gree**-foh
rusty	oxi**da**do	oh-ksee-**dah**-doh		**de la lla**ve	deh lah yah-veh
safe	se**gu**ro	seh-**goo**-roh	thick	**grue**so	**grweh**-soh
salt *(water)*	sa**la**da	sah-**lah**-dah	thick *(liquids)*	es**pe**so	ehss-**peh**-soh
sea *(water)*	**de mar**	**deh mahr**	thin	del**ga**do	dehl-**gah**-doh
seized-up	a·ga·rro**ta**do	ah-gah-**rroh**-tah-doh	tight	a·pre**ta**do	ah-preh-**tah**-doh
shallow ("not much deep")	**po**co pro**fun**do	**poh**-koh proh-foon-doh	too much	de·ma**sia**do	deh-mah-**syah**-doh
			twisted	re·tor**ci**do	reh-tohr-**see**-doh
short	**cor**to	**kohr**-toh	up	a**rri**ba	ah-**rree**-bah
slow	des**pa**cio,	dehss-**pah**-syoh	upper	supe**rior**	soo-peh-**ryohr**
	lento	**lehn**-toh	used	u**sa**do	oo-sah-doh
small	pe**que**ño	peh-keh-nyoh	very	**muy**	**mwee**
smooth *(running)*	**sua**ve	**swah**-veh	vibrating	vi**bran**do	vee-**brahn**-doh
smooth *(surface)*	**li**so	**lee**-soh	weak	**dé**bil	**deh**-beel
split	par**ti**do	pahr-**tee**-doh	wet	mo**ja**do	moh-**hah**-doh
square	cua**dra**do	kwah-**drah**-doh	white	**blan**co	**blahn**-koh
sticky	pe·ga**jo**so	peh-gah-**hoh**-soh	with current	**con** co**rrien**te	**kohn** koh-**rryehn**-teh
stopped	pa**ra**do	pah-**rah**-doh	w/out current	**sin** co**rrien**te	**seen** koh-**rryehn**-teh
straight	**rec**to	**rehk**-toh	worn	gas**ta**do	gahss-**tah**-doh
strong	**fuer**te	**fwehr**-te	worse	pe**or**	peh-**ohr**

© 2000 Kathy Parsons, Spanish for Cruisers

Use these sentences to describe the problems you are having with your engine.

Engine won't start or is difficult to start.

The engine doesn't start.	**El** mo**tor** **no** a·**rran**·ca. **El** mo**tor** **no** **pren**·de.	**Ehl** moh-**tohr** **noh** ah-**rrahn**-kah. **Ehl** moh-**tohr** **noh** **prehn**-deh.
It is difficult to start the motor.	**Es** di**fí**·cil a·rran·**car** **el** mo**tor**.	**Ehss** dee-fee-seel ah-rrahn-**kahr** **ehl** moh-**tohr**.
The engine doesn't turn over (crank).	**El** mo**tor** **no** **gi**·ra.	**Ehl** moh-**tohr** **noh** hee-rah.
The engine turns over very slowly.	**El** mo**tor** **gi**·ra **muy** des·**pa**·cio.	**Ehl** moh-**tohr** hee-rah **mwee** dehss-**pah**-syoh.
The engine turns over but doesn't start.	**El** mo**tor** **gi**·ra **pe**·ro **no** a·**rran**·ca.	**Ehl** moh-**tohr** hee-rah **peh**-roh **noh** ah-**rrahn**-kah.

Engine runs poorly or dies.

The engine doesn't run well in idle.	**El** mo**tor** **no** fun·cio·na **bien** **en** **ba**·ja re·vo·lu·**ción**.	**Ehl** moh-**tohr** **noh** foon-**syoh**-nah **byehn** **ehn** **bah**-hah reh-voh-loo-**syohn**.
The engine doesn't have power.	**El** mo**tor** **no** **tie**·ne po·**ten**·cia.	**Ehl** moh-**tohr** **noh** **tyeh**-neh poh-**tehn**-syah.
The engine loses power.	**El** mo**tor** **pier**·de po·**ten**·cia.	**Ehl** moh-**tohr** **pyehr**-deh poh-**tehn**-syah.
The engine stops (stalls).	**El** mo**tor** **se** **pa**·ra.	**Ehl** moh-**tohr** **seh** **pah**-rah.
The engine has low compression.	**El** mo**tor** **tie**·ne com·pre·**sión** **ba**·ja.	**Ehl** moh-**tohr** **tyeh**-neh kohm-preh-**syohn** **bah**-hah.
The engine misfires.	**El** mo**tor** **fa**·lla.	**Ehl** moh-**tohr** **fah**-yah.
The engine has blow-by.	**El** mo**tor** **tie**·ne **fu**·gas **de** com·pre·**sión**.	**Ehl** moh-**tohr** **tyeh**-neh **foo**-gahss **deh** kohm-preh-**syohn**.

© 2000 Kathy Parsons, Spanish for Cruisers

English	Spanish	Pronunciation
The valve sticks.	**La vál**vu·la **se pe**ga.	Lah **vahl**-voo-lah **seh peh**-gah.
The valve is stuck.	**La vál**vu·la es**tá** pe·**ga**da.	Lah **vahl**-voo-lah ehss-**tah** peh-**gah**-dah.

Engine overheats and/or no exhaust water.

English	Spanish	Pronunciation
The engine is too hot.	**El mo·tor** es**tá** de·ma·**sia**·do ca·**lien**·te.	Ehl moh-**tohr** ehss-**tah** deh-mah-**syah**-doh kah-**lyehn**-teh.
The engine overheats.	**El mo·tor se** re·ca·**lien**·ta.	Ehl moh-**tohr seh** reh-kah-**lyehn**-tah.
The engine overheats with a heavy load.	**El mo·tor se** re·ca·**lien**·ta con **u·na car**ga pe·**sa**da.	Ehl moh-**tohr se** reh-kah-**lyehn**-tah **kohn** oo-nah **kahr**-gah peh-**sah**-dah.
The engine overheats at idle.	**El mo·tor se** re·ca·**lien**·ta en **ba**·ja.	Ehl moh-**tohr se** reh-kah-**lyehn**-tah **ehn** bah-hah.
No exhaust water comes out.	**No sa**·le **a**·gua **del** es·**ca**·pe.	Noh sah-leh ah-gwah **dehl** ehss-**kah**-peh.
Little exhaust water comes out.	**Sa**·le **po**·ca **a**·gua **del** es·**ca**·pe.	Sah-leh **poh**-kah ah-gwah **dehl** ehss-**kah**-peh.

Fuel problems

English	Spanish	Pronunciation
The fuel is dirty.	**El** com·bus·**ti**·ble es**tá su**·cio.	Ehl kohm-booss-**tee**-bleh ehss-**tah soo**-syoh.
The fuel is contaminated.	**El** com·bus·**ti**·ble es**tá** con·ta·mi·**na**do.	Ehl kohm-booss-**tee**-bleh ehss-**tah** kohn-tah-mee-**nah**-doh.
There is water in the fuel.	**Hay a**·gua **en el** com·bus·**ti**·ble.	Eye ah-gwah **ehn ehl** kohm-booss-**tee**-bleh.
The engine is flooded.	**El mo·tor** es**tá** a·**ho·ga**do.	Ehl moh-**tohr** ehss-**tah** ah-oh-**gah**-doh.
There is air in the fuel system.	**Hay ai**·re **en el** sis·**te**·ma **de** com·bus·**ti**·ble.	Eye **eye**-reh **ehn ehl** seess-**teh**-mah **deh** kohm-booss-**tee**-bleh.
They poured gasoline instead of diesel in the tank.	E·**cha**·ron ga·so·**li**·na **en vez de** gas·**oil en el tan**·que.	Eh-**chah**-rohn gah-soh-**lee**-nah **en vehss deh** gahss-**oyl ehn ehl tahn**-keh.

© 2000 Kathy Parsons, Spanish for Cruisers

Use these sentences to describe the problems you are having with your engine.

Low oil pressure, burns oil, or oil level rising

The oil pressure is very low.	**La** pre·**sión del** a·cei·te es·**tá muy ba**·ja.	**Lah** preh-**syohn dehl** ah-**say**-teh ehss-**tah mwee bah**-hah.
The oil pressure has fallen little by little.	**La** pre·**sión del** a·cei·te **ha** ba·ja·do **po**·co a **po**·co.	**Lah** preh-**syohn dehl** ah-**say**-teh **ah** bah-**hah**-doh **poh**-koh ah **poh**-koh.
The oil pressure fell rapidly.	**La** pre·**sión del** a·cei·te ba·**jó rá**·pi·da·men·te.	**Lah** preh-**syohn dehl** ah-**say**-teh bah-**hoh rah**-pee-dah-**mehn**-teh.
The oil level is rising.	**El** ni·**vel del** a·cei·te es·**tá** su·**bien**·do.	**Ehl** nee-**vehl dehl** ah-**say**-teh ehss-**tah** soo-**byehn**-doh.
There is water in the oil in the crankcase.	**Hay** a·gua **en el** a·cei·te **del cár**·ter.	**Eye** ah-gwah **ehn ehl** ah-**say**-teh **dehl kahr**-tehr.
There is diesel fuel in the oil in the crankcase.	**Hay** gas·oil **(die**·sel**) en el** a·cei·te **del cár**·ter.	**Eye** gahss-oil **(dee**-sehl**) ehn ehl** ah-**say**-teh **dehl kahr**-tehr.
The engine consumes too much oil.	**El** mo·**tor** con·su·me de·ma·sia·do a·cei·te.	**Ehl** moh-**tohr** kohn-soo-meh deh-mah-**syah**-doh ah-**say**-teh.
The engine consumes 1 liter of oil every 10 hours.	**El** mo·**tor** con·su·me **un li**·tro **de** a·cei·te ca·da **diez ho**·ras.	**Ehl** moh-**tohr** kohn-soo-meh **oon lee**-troh **deh** ah-**say**-teh **kah**-dah **dyehss oh**-rahss.

© 2000 Kathy Parsons, Spanish for Cruisers

Engine smokes.		
Black smoke comes out.	Sale humo negro.	Sah-leh oo-moh neh-groh.
Blue smoke comes out.	Sale humo azul.	Sah-leh oo-moh ah-sool.
White smoke comes out.	Sale humo blanco.	Sah-leh oo-moh blahn-koh.

Leaks, cracks, and holes		
It has an oil leak at the ...	Tiene una fuga de aceite en el ...	Tyeh-neh oo-nah foo-gah deh ah-say-teh ehn ehl ...
It has a water leak at the ...	Tiene una fuga de agua en el ...	Tyeh-neh oo-nah foo-gah deh ah-gwah ehn ehl ...
It has a fuel leak at the ...	Tiene una fuga de combustible en el ...	Tyeh-neh oo-nah foo-gah deh kohm-booss-tee-bleh ehn ehl ...
... is plugged.	... está tapado. *	... ehss-tah tah-pah-doh.
... is worn.	... está gastado. *	... ehss-tah gahss-tah-doh.
There is a crack in the ...	Hay una rajadura en el ...	Eye oo-nah rah-hah-doo-rah ehn ehl ...
There is a hole in the ...	Hay un agujero en el ...	Eye oon ah-goo-heh-roh ehn ehl ....
... is loose (not tight enough).	... está flojo. *	... ehss-tah floh-hoh.
... is loose (unattached).	... está suelto. *	... ehss-tah swehl-toh.
... is broken.	... está roto. *	... ehss-tah roh-toh.
... is corroded.	... está corroído. *	... ehss-tah koh-rroh-ee-doh.
... is burnt.	... está quemado. *	... ehss-tah keh-mah-doh.

Está ... (without a noun before it) means "It is ...". eg. Está tapado = It is plugged.

© 2000 Kathy Parsons, Spanish for Cruisers

Use these sentences to describe the problems you are having with your engine.

Boat won't move – transmission, prop

English	Spanish	Pronunciation
The engine runs but the boat doesn't go forward.	El motor trabaja pero el barco no avanza.	Ehl moh-tohr trah-bah-hah peh-roh ehl bahr-koh noh ah-vahn-sah.
The propeller shaft does not turn in forward gear. **	El eje de la hélice no gira en marcha adelante.	Ehl eh-heh deh lah eh-lee-seh noh hee-rah ehn mahr-chah ah-deh-lahn-teh.
The propeller shaft does not turn in reverse. **	El eje de la hélice no gira en reversa.	Ehl eh-heh deh lah eh-lee-seh noh hee-rah ehn reh-vehr-sah.
The propeller shaft turns but the boat does not move. **	El eje de la hélice gira pero el barco no avanza.	Ehl eh-heh deh lah eh-lee-seh hee-rah peh-roh ehl bahr-koh noh ah-vahn-sah.
The propeller is damaged.	La hélice está dañada. La propela está dañada.	Lah eh-lee-seh ehss-tah dah-nyah-dah. Lah proh-peh-lah ehss-tah dah-nyah-dah.
The propeller shaft is bent. **	El eje de la hélice está doblado.	Ehl eh-heh deh lah eh-lee-seh ehss-tah doh-blah-doh.

** *In Mexico use* **la fle**cha *(lah fleh-chah) in place of* **el e**je *for "the shaft".*

© 2000 Kathy Parsons, Spanish for Cruisers

Noises and vibration

English	Español	Pronunciation
The engine makes noise (knocks).	**El** mo·**tor** ha·ce **rui**·do.	**Ehl** moh-**tohr** ah-seh **rwee**-doh.
The engine is vibrating more than normal.	**El** mo·**tor** es·**tá** vi·**bran**·do **más de lo** nor·**mal**.	**Ehl** moh-**tohr** ehss-**tah** vee-**brahn**-doh **mahss deh loh** nohr-**mahl**.

Spark plug problems

English	Español	Pronunciation
It doesn't spark.	**No tie**·ne **chis**·pa.	Noh **tyeh**-neh **cheess**-pah.
The spark plug is carbonned.	**La** bu·**jí**·a es·**tá** car·bo·ni·**za**·da.	**Lah** boo-**hee**-ah ehss-**tah** kahr-boh-nee-**sah**-dah.
The spark plug is burned.	**La** bu·**jí**·a es·**tá** que·**ma**·da.	**Lah** boo-**hee**-ah ehss-**tah** keh-**mah**-dah.
The spark plug is wet.	**La** bu·**jí**·a es·**tá** mo·**ja**·da.	**Lah** boo-**hee**-ah ehss-**tah** moh-**hah**-dah.
The spark plug is broken.	**La** bu·**jí**·a es·**tá** **ro**·ta.	**Lah** boo-**hee**-ah ehss-**tah** **roh**-tah.
The spark plug is fouled.	**La** bu·**jí**·a es·**tá** con·ta·mi·**na**·da. **La** bu·**jí**·a es·**tá** en·chum·**ba**·da. *(Venezuela)*	**Lah** boo-**hee**-ah ehss-**tah** kohn-tah-mee-**nah**-dah. **Lah** boo-**hee**-ah ehss-**tah** ehn-choom-**bah**-dah.

Outboard problems

English	Español	Pronunciation
It was submerged. in salt water.	**Fue** hun·**di**·do **en a**·gua sa·**la**·da.	**Fweh** oon-**dee**-doh **ehn** ah-gwah sah-**lah**-dah.
It doesn't plane any more with 2 people...	**Ya no** pla·**ne**·a **con dos** per·**so**·nas.	**Yah noh** plah-**neh**-ah **kohn dohss** pehr-**soh**-nahss.

© 2000 Kathy Parsons, Spanish for Cruisers

When can you give me an estimate?	¿**Cuán**do **pue**de **dar**me **un** presu**pues**to?	**Kwahn**-doh **pweh**-deh **dahr**-meh **oon** preh-soo-**pwehss**-toh?
When can you tell me if you can repair this?	¿**Cuán**do **pue**de de**cir**me **si pue**de repa**rar es**to?	**Kwahn**-doh **pweh**-deh deh-**seer**-meh **see pweh**-deh reh-pah-**rahr ehss**-toh?
How much time do you need to repair this?	¿**Cuán**to **tiem**po ne**ce·si·ta pa**ra repa**rar es**to?	**Kwahn**-toh **tyehm**-poh neh-seh-**see**-tah pah-rah reh-pah-**rahr ehss**-toh?
When can you finish the job?	¿**Cuán**do **pue**de termi**nar el** tra·**ba**·jo?	**Kwahn**-doh **pweh**-deh tehr-mee-**nahr ehl** trah-**bah**-hoh?
How much time to do you need to finish the work?	¿**Cuán**to **tiem**po ne**ce·si·ta pa**ra termi**nar el** tra·ba·jo?	**Kwahn**-toh **tyehm**-poh neh-seh-**see**-tah pah-rah tehr-mee-**nahr ehl** trah-**bah**-hoh?
When can you begin the work?	¿**Cuán**do **pue**de empe**zar el** tra·**ba**·jo?	**Kwah**-doh **pweh**-deh ehm-peh-**sahr ehl** trah-**bah**-hoh?
I need to leave on Monday.	Ne·ce·**si**·to sa·lir **el lu**·nes.	Neh-seh-**see**-toh sah-**leer ehl loo**-nehss.
Is it possible to repair this today?	¿**Es** po·**si**·ble repa·**rar es**to **hoy**?	**Ehss** poh-**see**-bleh reh-pah-**rahr ehss**-toh **oy**?
Is it possible to repair this for tomorrow?	¿**Es** po·**si**·ble repa·**rar es**to **pa**·ra ma·**ña**·na?	**Ehss** poh-**see**-bleh reh-pah-**rahr ehss**-toh **pah**-rah mah-**nyah**-nah?
I'll come (back) tomorrow.	**Ven**·go ma·**ña**·na.	**Vehn**-goh mah-**nyah**-nah.
Is it ready?	¿Es·**tá lis**·to?	Ehss-**tah leess**-toh?

© 2000 Kathy Parsons, Spanish for Cruisers

What repair is needed?

What repair does the motor need?	¿**Qué** a·**rre**·glo ne·ce·si·ta **el** mo·**tor**?	**Keh** ah-**rreh**-gloh neh-seh-**see**-tah **ehl** moh-**tohr**?
Can you write down the repair it needs?	¿**Pue**·de es·cri·**bir el** a·**rre**·glo **que** ne·ce·si·ta?	**Pweh**-deh ehss-kree-**beer ehl** ah-**rreh**-gloh **keh** neh-seh-**see**-tah?
I need an estimate first.	Ne·ce·si·to **un** pre·su·**puess**·to pri·**me**·ro.	Neh-seh-**see**-toh **oon** preh-soo-**pwehss**-toh pree-**meh**-roh.
What is the problem?	¿**Cuál es el** pro·**ble**·ma?	**Kwahl** ehss **ehl** proh-**bleh**-mah?
Which parts do you need to replace?	¿**Qué pie**·zas ne·ce·si·ta cam·**biar**?	**Keh pyeh**-sahss neh-seh-**see**-tah kahm-**byahr**?

What will it cost?

How much does it cost to repair this?	¿**Cuán**·to **cues**·ta re·pa·**rar es**·to?	**Kwahn**-toh **kwehss**-tah reh-pah-**rahr ehss**-toh?
How much do the parts cost?	¿**Cuán**·to **cues**·tan **las pie**·zas?	**Kwahn**-toh **kwehss**-tahn **lahss pyeh**-sahss?
How much does the labor cost?	¿**Cuán**·to **cues**·ta **la ma**·no **de** o·bra?	**Kwahn**-toh **kwehss**-tah **lah mah**-noh **deh** oh-brah?
How much does a new one cost?	¿**Cuán**·to **cues**·ta com·**prar** o·tro **nue**·vo?	**Kwahn**-toh **kwehss**-tah kohm-**prahr** oh-troh **nweh**-voh?
How much does a rebuilt one cost?	¿**Cuán**·to **cues**·ta com·**prar** o·tro re·cons·**truí**·do?	**Kwahn**-toh **kwehss**-tah kohm-**prahr** oh-troh reh-kohn-**strwee**-doh?
Where can I buy a used one?	¿**Dón**·de **pue**·do com·**prar** u·no u·**sa**·do?	**Dohn**-deh **pweh**-doh kohm-**prahr** oo-noh oo-**sah**-doh?

© 2000 Kathy Parsons, Spanish for Cruisers

Getting parts		
Which parts do you need to replace?	¿**Qué pie**zas ne·ce·si·ta cam**biar**?	**Keh pyeh**-sahss neh-seh-**see**-tah kahm-**byahr**?
Do you have the part?	¿**Tie**ne **el** re·**pues**to?	**Tyeh**-neh **ehl** reh-**pwehss**-toh?
Can you get the part?	¿**Pue**de con·se**guir el** re·**pues**to?	**Pweh**-deh kohn-seh-**gheer ehl** reh-**pwehss**-toh?
Can you order the part?	¿**Pue**de or·de**nar el** re·**pues**to?	**Pweh**-deh ohr-deh-**nahr ehl** reh-**pwehss**-toh?
When are you going to receive the part?	¿**Cuán**do **va a** re·ci**bir el** re·**pues**to?	**Kwahn**-doh **vah ah** reh-see-**beer ehl** reh-**pwehss**-toh?
Is it sure that you can get the part?	¿**Es** se·**gu**ro **que** con·si·gue us·**ted el** re·**pues**to?	**Ehss** seh-**goo**-roh **keh** kohn-**see**-gheh ooss-**tehd ehl** reh-**pwehss**-toh?
Can you get the parts for tomorrow?	¿**Pue**de con·se**guir las pie**zas **pa**·ra ma·**ña**·na?	**Pweh**-deh kohn-seh-**gheer lahss pyeh**-sahss **pah-rah** mah-**nyah**-nah?
Where can I get the part?	**Dón**·de **pue**·do con·se**guir el** re·**pues**to?	**Dohn**-deh **pweh**-doh kohn-seh-**gheer ehl** reh-**pwehss**-toh?
Is there another place where I can get this?	¿**Hay** o·tro lu·**gar don**·de **pue**·do con·se**guir es**·to?	**Eye oh**-troh loo-**gahr dohn**-deh **pweh**-doh kohn-seh-**gheer ehss**-toh?
Can you write the name?	¿**Pue**·de es·cri**bir el nom**·bre?	**Pweh**-deh ehss-kree-**beer ehl nohm**-breh?

© 2000 Kathy Parsons, Spanish for Cruisers

These phrases are useful when you need to make arrangements for a mechanic to come out to your boat.

Can you come to the boat?		
Can you come to my boat?	¿Puede venir a mi barco?	Pweh-deh veh-neer ah mee bahr-koh?
Can you go out to my boat?	¿Puede ir a mi barco?	Pweh-deh eer ah mee bahr-koh?
When ...?	¿Cuándo ...?	Kwahn-doh ...?
At what time?	¿A qué hora ....?	Ah keh oh-rah ...?
I can pass by for you at the dock at 9.	Puedo pasar por usted en el muelle a las nueve.	Pweh-doh pah-sahr porh ooss-tehd ehn ehl mweh-yeh ah lahss nweh-veh.
Can you be at the dock at 9?	¿Puede estar en el muelle a las nueve?	Pweh-deh ehss-tahr ehn ehl mweh-yeh ah lahss nweh-veh?
When are you going to return to the boat?	¿Cuándo regresa al barco?	Kwahn-doh reh-greh-sah ahl bahr-koh?

My boat is anchored in ...	Mi barco está anclado en	Mee bahr-koh ehss-tah ahn-klah-doh ehn ...
My boat is at the dock.	Mi barco está en el muelle.	Mee bahr-koh ehss-tah ehn ehl mweh-yeh.
My boat is in the boatyard.	Mi barco está en el varadero.	Mee bahr-koh ehss-tah ehn ehl vah-rah-deh-roh.
I can bring my boat to the dock.	Puedo llevar mi barco al muelle.	Pweh-doh yeh-vahr mee bahr-koh ahl mweh-yeh.

© 2000 Kathy Parsons, Spanish for Cruisers

Do you have a radio?	¿Tiene radio?	Tyeh-neh rah-dyoh?
I stand by on channel 16.	Escucho **en el** canal 16 (**diez y seis**).	Ehss-koo-choh **ehn ehl** kah-**nahl dyehss ee sayss.**
Can you call me tomorrow at 9?	¿Puede lla**mar**me ma**ña**na **a las nue**ve?	Pweh-deh yah-**mahr**-meh mah-**nyah**-nah **ah lahss nweh**-veh?

Can you fix it on the boat?

Can you repair this on the boat?	¿Puede reparar esto **en el** barco?	Pweh-deh reh-pah-**rahr** ehss-toh **ehn ehl** bahr-koh?
Do I need to remove the motor from the boat?	¿Necesito sa**car el** mo**tor del** barco?	Neh-seh-see-toh sah-**kahr ehl** moh-**tohr dehl** bahr-koh?
It is not possible to remove the motor from the boat.	**No es** posible sa**car el** mo**tor del** barco.	**Noh ehss** poh-**see**-bleh sah-**kahr ehl** moh-**tohr dehl** bahr-koh.
I prefer to repair the motor on the boat if it is possible.	Pre**fie**ro repa**rar el** mo**tor en el** barco **si es** posible.	Preh-**fyeh**-roh reh-pah-**rahr ehl** moh-**tohr ehn ehl** bahr-koh **see ehss** poh-**see**-bleh.
Do I need to haul the boat?	¿Necesito sa**car el** barco?	Neh-seh-see-toh sah-**kahr ehl** bahr-koh?

© 2000 Kathy Parsons, Spanish for Cruisers

compressor	el	com·pre·**sor**	kohm-preh-**sohr**
condenser	el	con·den·sa·**dor**	kohn-dehn-sah-**dohr**
copper tubing	la	tu·be·**rí**·a **de co**·bre	too-beh-**ree**-ah **deh koh**-breh
discharge line	el	**tu**·bo **de** des·**car**·ga	**too**-boh **deh** dehss-**kahr**-gah
evaporator	el	e·va·po·ra·**dor**	eh-vah-poh-rah-**dohr**
expansion valve	la	**vál**·vu·la **de** ex·pan·**sión**	**vahl**-voo-lah **deh** ehkss-pahn-**syohn**
filter	el	**fil**·tro	**feel**-troh
gas (freon)	el	**gas (fre**·on)	**gahss (free**-ohn)
heat exchanger	el	in·ter·cam·bia·**dor de** ca·**lor**	een-tehr-kahm-byah-**dohr deh** kah-**lohr**
high pressure cut-out	el	in·te·rrup·**tor de al**·ta pre·**sión**	een-teh-roop-**tohr deh ahl**-tah preh-**syohn**
high pressure side	el	**la**·do **de al**·ta pre·**sión**	**lah**-doh **deh ahl**-tah preh-**syohn**
holding plate	la	**pla**·ca a·cu·mu·la·**do**·ra	**plah**-kah ah-koo-moo-lah-**doh**-rah
hose	la	man·**gue**·ra	mahn-**gheh**-rah
insulation	el	ais·la·**mien**·to	eyess-lah-**myehn**-toh
leak-detector	el	de·tec·**tor de fu**·gas	deh-tehk-**tohr deh foo**-gahss
liquid	el	**lí**·qui·do	**lee**-kee-doh
low pressure cut-out	el	in·te·rrup·**tor de ba**·ja pre·**sión**	een-teh-rroop-**tohr deh bah**-hah preh-**syohn**
low pressure side	el	**la**·do **de ba**·ja pre·**sión**	**lah**-doh **deh bah**-hah preh-**syohn**

© 2000 Kathy Parsons, Spanish for Cruisers

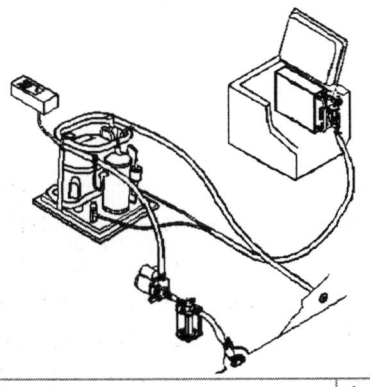

pipe	el	**tu**·bo	**too**-boh
R-12	el	**R-12** (**do**·ce)	**Eh**-reh **doh**-seh
R-22	el	**R-22** (vein·ti·**dós**)	**Eh**-reh vayn-tee-**dohss**
receiver	el	re·cep·**tor**	reh-sehp-**tohr**
drier	el	se·ca·**dor**	seh-kah-**dohr**
refrigerant	el	re·fri·ge·**ran**·te	reh-free-heh-**rahn**-teh
refrigeration gauges	los	ma·**nó**·me·tros **de** re·fri·ge·ra·**ción**	mah-**noh**-meh-trohss **deh** reh-free-heh-rah-**syohn**
refrigeration oil	el	a·**cei**·te **de** re·fri·ge·ra·**ción**	ah-**say**-teh **deh** reh-free-heh-rah-**syohn**
sight-glass	el	vi·**sor**	vee-**sohr**
	el	**tu**·bo **de** vi·drio **de** ni·**vel**	**too**-boh **deh** **vee**-dryoh **deh** nee-**vehl**
thermostat	el	ter·mos·**ta**·to	tehr-mohss-**tah**-toh

© 2000 Kathy Parsons, Spanish for Cruisers

vacuum pump	la	**bom**ba **de** va·**cí**o	**bohm**-bah **deh** vah-**see**-oh
pressure	la	pre·**sión**	preh-**syohn**
vacuum	el	va·**cí**o	vah-**see**-oh
temperature	la	tem·pe·ra·**tu**·ra	tehm-peh-rah-**too**-rah
degrees	los	**gra**·dos	**grah**-dohss

Can you ...?	¿**Pue**de...?	Pweh-deh...?
...check out the system	...re·vi·**sar** **el** sis·**te**·ma	reh-vee-**sahr** **ehl** seess-**teh**-mah
...check if there are leaks	...re·vi·**sar** **si** **hay** **fu**·gas	reh-vee-**sahr** **see** **eye** foo-gahss
...check the level of refrigerant	...re·vi·**sar** **el** ni·**vel** **de** re·fri·ge·**ran**·te	reh-vee-**sahr** **ehl** nee-**vehl** **deh** reh-free-heh-**rahn**-teh
...charge the system	...car·**gar** **el** sis·**te**·ma	kahr-**gahr** **ehl** sees-**teh**-mah
...add refrigerant	...e·**char** re·fri·ge·**ran**·te	poh-**nehr** reh-free-heh-**rahn**-teh
...open the valve a little	...a·**brir** **la** **vál**·vu·la **un** **po**·co	ah-**breer** **la** vahl-voo-lah **oon** **poh**-koh
...replace the drier	...cam·**biar** **el** se·ca·**dor**	kahm-**byahr** **ehl** seh-kah-**dohr**
...fix the leaks	...a·rre·**glar** **las** **fu**·gas	ah-rreh-**glahr** **lahss** foo-gahss
...purge the system	...pur·**gar** **el** sis·**te**·ma	poor-**gahr** **ehl** seess-**teh**-mah

© 2000 Kathy Parsons, Spanish for Cruisers

Trouble-shooting		
It isn't cooling.	No enfría.	**Noh** ehn-**free**-ah.
It isn't freezing.	No congela.	**Noh** kohn-**heh**-lah.
It has a leak.	**Tie**ne una **fu**ga.	**Tyeh**-neh oo-nah **foo**-gah.
It is running more than normal.	Tra·ba·ja **más de lo** nor·**mal**.	Trah-**bah**-hah **mahss deh loh** nohr-**mahl**.
It is losing refrigerant.	**Pier**de refrigerante.	**Pyehr**-deh reh-free-heh-**rahn**-teh.
It doesn't have any refrigerant.	**No tie**ne refrigerante.	**No tyeh**-neh reh-free-heh-**rahn**-teh.
It doesn't have enough refrigerant.	No **tie**ne bas**tan**te refrigerante.	**Noh tyeh**-neh bahss-**tahn**-teh reh-free-heh-**rahn**-teh.
It has too much refrigerant.	**Tie**ne de·ma·**sia**do refrigerante.	**Tyeh**-neh deh-mah-**syah**-doh reh-free-heh-**rahn**-teh.
It's full.	Es**tá lle**no.	Ehss-**tah yeh**-noh.
It is making a noise.	**Ha**ce **un rui**do.	Ah-seh **oon rwee**-doh.

© 2000 Kathy Parsons, Spanish for Cruisers

It is cold.	Está **frí**·o.	Ehss-**tah free**-oh.
It is cool.	Está **fres**·co.	Ehss-**tah frehss**-koh.
It is lukewarm.	Es·**tá ti**·bio.	Ess-**tah tee**-byoh.
It is hot.	Está ca·**lien**·te.	Ess-tah kah-**lyehn**-teh.
The motor isn't running.	**El** mo·**tor no** fun·**cio**·na.	**Ehl** moh-**tohr noh** foon-**syoh**-nah.
The sight glass is empty.	**El** vi·**sor** está va·**cí**·o.	**Ehl** vee-**sohr** ehss-**tah** vah-**see**-oh.
The sight glass is full of liquid.	**El** vi·**sor** está **lle**·no **de lí**·qui·do.	**Ehl** vee-**sohr** ehss-**tah yeh**-noh **deh** lee-kee-doh.
The sight glass has bubbles.	**El** vi·**sor tie**·ne bur·**bu**·jas.	**Ehl** vee-**sohr tyeh**-neh boor-**boo**-hahss.

Where I learned my Spanish...

I studied Spanish in school starting with the 3rd grade, but my fluency comes from my stint with the Peace Corps in Nicaragua in the 1970's. I worked with a small-business cooperative in a small Nicaraguan town. (The average business loan was about $30US.) I worked on a variety of projects – potable water, adult literacy, latrines, housing loans and other community services. I also taught English to high school students. After the Peace Corps, I worked on some Latin American development projects, translating reports from English to Spanish and designing questionnaires in Spanish.

Of course, almost twenty years later, when I went back to Latin America by boat, I had to learn some new vocabulary. In the countries I have cruised to, I have found no shortage of Spanish "teachers" to help fill in my boating and mechanical vocabulary. I found helpful dock masters, hardware clerks, officials, boatyard owners, mechanics, agents, canvas makers, and just plain nice people wherever I cruised. They were flattered that I was so interested in their language and quite eager to help. Sometimes, they would even sit in the back of the classes I gave to cruisers and watch me teach!

I complained to a friend recently that I still frequently make mistakes in Spanish, particularly when I'm tired. He replied "So what! You make mistakes in English too." He had a point... So, don't beat yourself up about your Spanish – just get out there and speak!

© 2000 Kathy Parsons, Spanish for Cruisers

power cable	el	**ca**ble **de** alimenta**ción**	**kah**-bleh **deh** ah-lee-mehn-tah-**syohn**
connector	el	conec**tor**	koh-nehk-**tohr**
microphone	el	mi**cró**fono	mee-**kroh**-foh-noh
keyboard, keypad	el	te**cla**do	teh-**klah**-doh
screen	la	pan**ta**lla	pahn-**tah**-yah
radio call sign	el la	indi**ca**tivo **de** lla**ma**da contra**se**ña	een-dee-kah-**tee**-voh **deh** yah-**mah**-dah kohn-trah-**seh**-nyah
frequency	la	fre**cuen**cia	freh-**kwehn**-syah
marine frequency	la	fre**cuen**cia ma**ri**na	freh-**kwehn**-syah mah-**ree**-nah
channel	el	ca**nal**	kah-**nahl**
signal	el	se**ñal**	seh-**nyahl**
interference	la	interfe**ren**cia	een-tehr-feh-**rehn**-syah
ham radio operator	el	radioaficio**na**do	rah-dyoh-ah-fee-syoh-**nah**-doh
stand-by	el	es**ta**do **de** es**cu**cha	ehss-**tah**-doh **deh** ehss-**koo**-chah
low power	la	po**ten**cia **ba**ja	poh-**tehn**-syah **bah**-hah
high power	la	po**ten**cia **al**ta	poh-**tehn**-syah **ahl**-tah
watts	los	**watts**	**wahts**
I can't transmit		**No pue**do transmi**tir.**	**Noh pweh**-doh trahnss-mee-**teer.**
I can't receive.		**No pue**do reci**bir.**	**Noh pweh**-doh reh-see-**beer.**
There's a lot of interference.		**Hay mu**cha interfe**ren**cia.	**Eye moo**-chah een-teh-feh-**rehn**-syah.

© 2000 Kathy Parsons, Spanish for Cruisers

Other Electronics

anemometer	el	anemómetro	ah-neh-**moh**-meh-troh
autopilot	el	piloto automático	pee-**loh**-toh ow-toh-**mah**-tee-koh
compass	el	com**pás**	kohm-**pahss**
	la	**brú**jula	**broo**-hoo-lah
computer	el	computa**dor**	kohm-poo-tah-**dohr**
speed log	la	corre**de**ra	koh-rreh-**deh**-rah
speedometer	el	velo**cí**metro	veh-loh-**see**-meh-troh
depthsounder	el	sonda**dor**	sohn-dah-**dohr**
	la	**son**da	**sohn**-dah
	el	profun**dí**metro	proh-foon-**dee**-meh-troh
GPS	el	**GPS**	**heh peh eh**-seh
printer	la	impre**so**ra	eem-preh-**soh**-rah
radar	el	ra**dar**	rah-**dahr**
radar reflector	el	reflec**tor** de ra**dar**	reh-flehk-**tohr deh** rah-**dahr**
transducer	el	trans**duc**tor	trahnss-dook-**tohr**
remote control	el	con**trol** re**mo**to	kohn-**trohl** reh-**moh**-toh
	el	con**trol** a dis**tan**cia	kohn-**trohl ah** deess-**tahn**-syah
solenoid	el	sole**noi**de	soh-leh-**noy**-deh
LCD screen	la	pan**ta**lla **LCD**	pahn-**tah**-yah **eh**-leh **seh deh**
output	la	sa**li**da	sah-**lee**-dah
watertight		**a prue**ba **de a**gua	**ah prweh**-bah **deh** ah-gwah

© 2000 Kathy Parsons, Spanish for Cruisers

Power generation			
battery charger	el	carga**dor de** bate**rí**a	kahr-gah-**dohr deh** bah-teh-**ree**-ah
generator	el	genera**dor**	heh-neh-rah-**dohr**
	la	**plan**ta e**léc**trica	**plahn**-tah eh-**lehk**-tree-kah
inverter	el	inverti**dor**	een-vehr-tee-**dohr**
	el	inver**sor**	een-vehr-**sohr**
solar panel	la	**pla**ca so**lar**	**plah**-kah soh-**lahr**
voltage regulator	el	regula**dor de** vol**ta**je	reh-goo-lah-**dohr deh** vohl-**tah**-heh
wind generator	el	genera**dor de vien**to	heh-neh-rah-**dohr deh vyehn**-toh
Electronic components			
condenser, capacitor	el	condensa**dor**	kohn-dehn-sah-**dohr**
converter	el	converti**dor**	kohn-vehr-tee-**dohr**
diode	el	**dio**do	**dyoh**-doh
relay	el	re**lé**	reh-**leh**
	el	**re**lay	**ree**-leh
resistor	el	resis**tor**	reh-seess-**tohr**
	la	resis**ten**cia	reh-seess-**tehn**-syah
transformer	el	transforma**dor**	trahnss-fohr-mah-**dohr**
inductor	el	induc**tor**	een-dook-**tohr**

© 2000 Kathy Parsons, Spanish for Cruisers

alarm	la	a·lar·ma	ah-**lahr**-mah
anchor light	la	**luz de** fon·de·o	**looss deh** fohn-**deh**-oh
bilge blower	el	ex·trac·**tor de las** sen·ti·nas	ehkss-trahk-**tohr deh lahss** sehn-**tee**-nahss
bilge pump	la	**bom**·ba **de** a·**chi**·que	**bohm**-bah **deh** ah-**chee**-keh
bilge pump, manual	la	**bom**·ba **de** a·**chi**·que ma·**nual**	**bohm**-bah **deh** ah-**chee**-keh mah-**nwahl**
burglar alarm system	el	sis·te·ma **de** a·lar·ma **con**·tra **ro**·bo	seess-**teh**-mah **deh** ah-**lahr**-mah **kohn**-trah **roh**-boh
clock	el	re·**loj**	reh-**loh**
electric switch	el	**switch**	ehss-**weetch**
	el	in·ter·rup·**tor**	een-teh-rroop-**tohr**
fan	el	ven·ti·la·**dor**	vehn-tee-lah-**dohr**
float switch	el	in·ter·rup·**tor** au·to·**má**·ti·co **pa**·ra **la bom**·ba **de** a·**chi**·que	een-teh-rroop-**tohr** ow-toh-**mah**-tee-koh **pah**-rah **lah bohm**-bah **deh** ah-**chee**-keh
fluorescent lamp	la	**lám**·pa·ra fluo·res·**cen**·te	**lahm**-pah-rah **floh**-rehss-**sehn**-teh
fluorescent tube	el	**tu**·bo fluo·res·**cen**·te	**too**-boh **floh**-rehss-**sehn**-teh
lamp	la	**lám**·pa·ra	**lahm**-pah-rah

© 2000 Kathy Parsons, Spanish for Cruisers

light	la	**luz**	**looss**
microwave	la	mi·cro·**on**·das	mee-kroh-**ohn**-dahss
navigation light	la	**luz de** na·ve·ga·**ción**	**looss deh** nah-veh-gah-**syohn**
pressure water pump	la	**bom**·ba **de a**·gua **a** pre·**sión**	**bohm**-bah **deh ah**-gwah **ah** preh-**syohn**
television	el	te·le·vi·**sor**	teh-leh-vee-**sohr**
	la	te·le·vi·**sión**	teh-leh-vee-**syohn**
water heater	el	ca·len·ta·**dor de a**·gua	kahl-lehn-tah-**dohr deh ah**-gwah
watermaker	la	de·sa·li·ni·za·**do**·ra	deh-sah-lee-nee-sah-**doh**-rah
	la	po·ta·bi·li·za·**do**·ra	poh-tah-bee-lee-sah-**doh**-rah
windlass	el	mo·li·**ne**·te	moh-lee-**neh**-teh
electric windlass	el	mo·li·**ne**·te e·**léc**·tri·co	moh-lee-**neh**-teh eh-**lehk**-tree-koh

Safety Equipment

lifejacket	el	cha·**le**·co sal·va·**vi**·das	chah-**leh**-koh sahl-vah-**vee**-dahss
flare	la	**luz de** ben·**ga**·la	**looss deh** behn-**gah**-lah
rocket	el	co·**he**·te	koh-**eh**-teh
smoke signal	el	se·**ñal de hu**·mo	seh-**nyahl deh** oo-moh
yellow dye	el	**tin**·te a·ma·**ri**·llo	**teen**-teh ah-mah-**ree**-yoh
fire extinguisher	el	ex·tin·gui·**dor**	ehkss-teen-gwee-**dohr**
liferaft	la	**bal**·sa sal·va·**vi**·das	**bahl**-sah sahl-vah-**vee**-dahss
EPIRB	el	**EPIRB**	eh-**peerb**
	el	trans·mi·**sor de** e·mer·**gen**·cia **pa**·ra **dar la** po·si·**ción**	trahnss-mee-**sohr deh** eh-mehr-**hehn**-syah **pah**-rah **dahr lah** poh-see-**syohn**

© 2000 Kathy Parsons, Spanish for Cruisers

I can't transmit	**No pue**do trans·mi·**tir**.	Noh **pweh**-doh trahnss-mee-**teer**.
I can't receive.	**No pue**do re·ci·**bir**.	Noh **pweh**-doh reh-see-**beer**.
The light doesn't light up.	**La luz no** en·**cien**·de.	**Lah looss noh** ehn-**syehn**-deh.
... works (functions) .	... fun·**cio**·na.	... foon-**syoh**-nah.
... doesn't work (function).	... **no** fun·**cio**·na.	... **noh** foon-**syoh**-nah.
... is bad.	... es·**tá ma**·lo.	... ehss-**tah mah**-loh.
...is good.	... es·**tá bue**·no.	... ehss-**tah bweh**-noh.
...is broken.	... es·**tá ro**·to.	... ehss-**tah roh**-toh.
...is disconnected.	... es·**tá** des·co·nec·**ta**·do.	... ehss-**tah** dehss-koh-nehk-**tah**-doh.
...is burnt.	... es·**tá** que·**ma**·do.	... ehss-**tah** keh-**mah**-doh.
It doesn't hold a charge.	No man·**tie**·ne **la car**·ga.	Noh mahn-**tyeh**-neh lah **kahr**-gah.
It's not getting current.	**No** re·ci·be co·**rrien**·te.	Noh reh-**see**-beh koh-**ryehn**-teh.
The voltage is 12.6 volts.	**El** vol·**ta**·je **es do**·ce **pun**·to **seis vol**·tios.	Ehl vohl-**tah**-heh **ehss doh**-seh **poon**-toh **sayss vohl**-tyohss.
The voltage should be 14.4 volts.	**El** vol·**ta**·je **de**·be **ser** ca·**tor**·ce **pun**·to **cua**·tro **vol**·tios.	Ehl vohl-**tah**-heh **deh**-beh **sehr** kah-**tohr**-seh **poon**-toh **kwah**-troh **vohl**-tyohss.
The resistence ...	La re·sis·**ten**·cia ...	Lah reh-seess-**tehn**-syah ...
... between the terminals ...	... **en**·tre **los** ter·mi·**na**·les ...	**ehn**-treh lohss tehr-mee-**nah**-lehss ...
... should be ...	... **de**·be **ser** ...	**deh**-beh **sehr** ...
... from 400 to 1000 ohms.	... **de** cua·tro·**cien**·tos **a mil ohms**.	deh kwah-troh-**syehn**-tohss **ah meel ohmss**.

© 2000 Kathy Parsons, Spanish for Cruisers

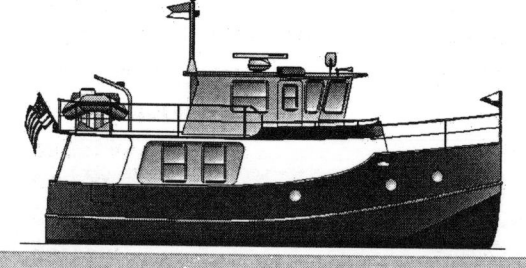

"Velero, Velero, Velero ..."
(Sailboat, Sailboat, Sailboat...)

This is a common way that sailboats are hailed on the VHF radio – they may be calling you!

Types of boats

boat	el	**bar**·co	**bahr**-koh
	el	**bo**·te	**boh**-teh
sailboat	el	ve·**le**·ro	veh-**leh**-roh
yacht	el	**ya**·te	**yah**-teh
motor yacht	el	**ya**·te **de** mo·**tor**	**yah**-teh **deh** moh-**tohr**
boat *("official" word)*	la	em·bar·ca·**ción**	ehm-bahr-kah-**syohn**
motorcruiser, cruiseship	el	cru·**ce**·ro	kroo-**seh**-roh
launch, boat	la	**lan**·cha	**lahn**-chah
dinghy	la	lan·**chi**·ta	lahn-**chee**-tah
canoe, small boat	la	ca·**no**·a	kah-**noh**-ah
raft	la	**bal**·sa	**bahl**-sah
rubber raft, inflatable	la	**bal**·sa **de** go·ma	**bahl**-sah **deh** goh-mah
	la	**bal**·sa **de** **hu**·le	**bahl**-sah **deh** oo-leh

© 2000 Kathy Parsons, Spanish for Cruisers

liferaft	la	**bal**·sa sal·va·**vi**·das	**bahl**-sah sahl-vah-**vee**-dahss
monohull	el	mo·no·**cas**·co	moh-noh-**kahss**-koh
catamaran	el	ca·ta·ma·**rán**	kah-tah-mah-**rahn**
trimaran	el	tri·ma·**rán**	tree-mah-**rahn**

Hull

hull	el	**cas**·co	**kahss**-koh
bow	la	**pro**·a	**proh**-ah
stern	la	**po**·pa	**poh**-pah
bottom	el	**fon**·do	**fohn**-doh
	la	ca·**rre**·na	kah-**rreh**-nah
keel	la	**qui**·lla	**kee**-yah
ballast	el	**las**·tre	**lahss**-treh
rudder	el	ti·**món**	tee-**mohn**
centerboard	la	**or**·za	**ohr**-sah
gelcoat	el	**gel**·coat	*English pronunciation*
side	el	cos·**ta**·do	kohss-**tah**-doh
	la	**ban**·da	**bahn**-dah
through-hull	el	pa·sa·**cas**·co	pah-sah-**kahss**-koh
transducer	el	trans·duc·**tor**	trahnss-dook-**tohr**
waterline	la	**lí**·ne·a **de** flo·ta·**ción**	**lee**-neh-ah **deh** floh-tah-**syohn**
below the waterline		de·**ba**·jo **de la lí**·ne·a **de** flo·ta·**ción**	deh-**bah**-hoh **deh lah lee**-neh-ah **deh** floh-tah-**syohn**

© 2000 Kathy Parsons, Spanish for Cruisers

Masts and Rigging

mast	el	**más**til	**mahss**-teel
	el	**pa**lo	**pah**-loh
main mast	el	**más**til ma**yor**	**mahss**-teel mah-**yohr**
mizzen mast	el	**más**til me**sa**na	**mahss**-teel meh-**sah**-nah
deck-stepped mast	el	**más**til en cu**bier**ta	**mahss**-teel **ehn** koo-**byehr**-tah
keel-stepped mast	el	**más**til en **qui**lla	**mahss**-teel **ehn** **kee**-yah
boom	la	bota**va**ra	boh-tah-**vah**-rah
rigging	la	**jar**cia	**hahr**-syah
	el	apa**re**jo	ah-pah-**reh**-hoh
stay	el	es**tay**	ehss-**teye**
forestay	el	es**tay** de **pro**a	ehss-**teye** deh **proh**-ah
backstay	la	**bur**da	**boor**-dah
shroud	el	o**ben**que	oh-**behn**-keh

© 2000 Kathy Parsons, Spanish for Cruisers

spreader	la	cru·**ce**·ta	kroo-**seh**-tah
roller furler	el	en·ro·lla·**dor**	ehn-roh-yah-**dohr**
spinnaker pole	el	tan·**gón**	tahn-**gohn**
turnbuckle	el	ten·**sor**	tehn-**sohr**

On deck			
deck	la	cu·**bier**·ta	koo-**byehr**-tah
cockpit	el	**cock**·pit	**kohk**-peet
	la	ba·**ñe**·ra	bah-**nyeh**-rah
hatch	la	es·co·ti·lla	ehss-koh-**tee**-yah
helm	el	ti·**món**	tee-**mohn**
cabin	la	ca·**bi**·na	kah-**bee**-nah
	el	ca·ma·**ro**·te	kah-mah-**roh**-teh
port (hole)	el	por·**ti**·llo	pohr-**tee**-yoh
pulpit	el	**púl**·pi·to	**pool**-pee-toh
stanchion	el	can·de·**le**·ro	kahn-deh-**leh**-roh
davits	el	pes·**can**·te	pehss-**kahn**-teh
cleat	la	cor·na·**mu**·sa	kohr-nah-**moo**-sah
handrail	la	pa·sa·**ma**·no	pah-sah-**mah**-noh
	la	a·ga·rra·**de**·ra	ah-gah-rrah-**deh**-rah
outboard bracket	el	so·**por**·te **pa**·ra mo·**tor** fue·ra de **bor**·da	soh-**pohr**-teh **pah**-rah moh-**tohr** fweh-rah **deh bohr**-dah

© 2000 Kathy Parsons, Spanish for Cruisers

Deck hardware			
hook	el	**gan**·cho	**gahn**-choh
ladder	la	es·**ca**·la	ehss-**kah**-lah
pulley	la	po·**le**·a	poh-**leh**-ah
track	el	ca·**rril**	kah-**rreel**
winch	el	**win**·che	**ween**-cheh
shackle	el	gri·**lle**·te	gree-**yeh**-teh

Ropes, lines, chain			
rope, line	el	**ca**·bo (<u>not</u> *ropa!*)	**kah**-boh
	la	**so**·ga (*ropa* means *clothes*)	**soh**-gah
	el	me·**ca**·te	meh-**kah**-teh
mooring line	el	**ca**·bo **de** a·**ma**·rre	**kah**-boh **deh** ah-**mah**-rreh
halyard	la	**dri**·za	**dree**-sah
sheet	la	es·**co**·ta	ehss-**koh**-tah
spring line	el	es·**prín**	ehss-**preen**
chain	la	ca·**de**·na	kah-**deh**-nah
chain link	el	es·la·**bón**	ehss-lah-**bohn**
thimble	el	guar·da·**ca**·bo	gwahr-dah-**kah**-boh
anchor	el	**an**·cla	**ahn**-klah
windlass	el	mo·li·**ne**·te	moh-lee-**neh**-teh

© 2000 Kathy Parsons, Spanish for Cruisers

Docks and anchorages

dock	el	**mue**·lle	**mweh**-yeh
slip	el	**pues**·to	**pwehss**-toh
	el	lu·**gar**	loo-**gahr**
mooring ball	el	**muer**·to (**de** a·**ma**·rre)	**mwehr**-toh (deh ah-**mah**-rreh)
anchorage	el	an·**cla**·je	ahn-**klah**-heh
	el	fon·de·a·**de**·ro	fohn-deh-ah-**deh**-roh
piling, post	el	pi·**lo**·te	pee-**loh**-teh
	el	**pos**·te	**pohss**-teh
cleat	la	cor·na·**mu**·sa	kohr-nah-**moo**-sah

Ropes, lines, anchors

rope, line	el	**ca**·bo	(not *ropa!*)	**kah**-boh
	la	**so**·ga	(*ropa* means *clothes*)	**soh**-gah
mooring line	el	**ca**·bo (**de** a·**ma**·rre)		**kah**-boh **deh** ah-**mah**-rreh)
spring line	el	es·**prín**		ehss-**preen**
anchor	el	**an**·cla		**ahn**-klah

Parts of boat

bow	la	**pro**·a	**proh**-ah
stern	la	**po**·pa	**poh**-pah
port side	el	cos·**ta**·do **de** ba·**bor**	kohss-**tah**-doh **deh** bah-**bohr**
starboard side	el	cos·**ta**·do **de** es·tri·**bor**	kohss-**tah**-doh **deh** ehss-tree-**bohr**
to dock, come alongside		a·tra·**car al mue**·lle	ah-trah-**kahr ahl mweh**-yeh
to dock port side to dock		a·tra·**car de** ba·**bor al mue**·lle	ah-trah-**kahr deh** bah-**bohr ahl mweh**-yeh

© 2000 Kathy Parsons, Spanish for Cruisers

to dock starboard side to dock	a·tra·**car de** es·tri·**bor al mue·**lle	ah-trah-**kahr** deh ehss-tree-**bohr** ahl mweh-yeh
to enter bow first	en·**trar de** la **pro·**a	ehn-**trahr** deh lah **proh**-ah
to enter stern first	en·**trar de** la **po·**pa	ehn-**trahr** deh lah poh-pah
to anchor first	an·**clar** pri·**me·**ro fon·de·**ar** pri·**me·**ro	ahn-**klahr** pree-meh-roh fohn-deh-**ahr** pre-meh-roh
to put out a stern anchor	po·**ner un an·**cla **de po·**pa	poh-**nehr** oon ahn-klah **deh** poh-pah

Give me the rope.	**Dé·**me **el ca·**bo.	Deh-meh **ehl** kah-boh.
Take the rope.	**To·**me **el ca·**bo.	Toh-meh **ehl** kah-boh.
Slack the rope.	A·**flo·**je **el ca·**bo.	Ah-floh-heh **ehl** kah-boh.
Cast off the rope.	**Lar·**gue **el ca·**bo.	Lahr-gheh **ehl** kah-boh.
Tie off the rope.	A·**ma·**rre **el ca·**bo.	Ah-mah-rreh **ehl** kah-boh.
Hold the rope.	A·**guan·**te **el ca·**bo.	Ah-gwahn-teh **ehl** kah-boh.
Fasten the rope.	**Fi·**je **el ca·**bo.	Fee-heh **ehl** kah-boh.

You may substitute "lo" (it) for
"el cabo" in any of these sentences.

Examples:
Dé·me·lo. (Give it to me.) *deh-meh-loh*
Tó·me·lo. (Take it.)   *toh-meh-loh*
Lár·gue·lo. (Cast it off.) *lahr-gheh-loh*

A little forward.	**un po·**co **ha·**cia a·de·**lan·**te.	oon poh-koh **ah-**syah ah-deh-**lahn**-teh.
A little backwards.	**un po·**co **ha·**cia a·**trás.**	oon poh-koh **ah-**syah ah-**trahss.**
To port.	**Al** ba·**bor.**	Ahl bah-**bohr.**
To starboard.	**Al** es·tri·**bor.**	Ahl ehss-tree-**bohr.**
Push.	Em·**pu·**je.	Ehm-**poo**-heh.
Pull.	**Ja·**le.	Hah-leh.

© 2000 Kathy Parsons, Spanish for Cruisers

Boatyard and facilities

boatyard	el	va·ra·**de**·ro	vah-rah-**deh**-roh
shipyard	el	as·ti·**lle**·ro	ahss-tee-**yeh**-roh
travelift	el	tra·ve·**lift**	"trah-veh-**leeft**"
travelift (50 tons)	el	tra·ve·**lift** de cin·**cuen**·ta to·ne·**la**·das	"trah-veh-**leeft**" **deh** seen-**kwehn**-tah toh-neh-**lah**-dahss
sling	la	es·**lin**·ga	ehss-**leen**-gah
crane, railway	la	**grú**·a	**groo**-ah
dock	el	**mue**·lle	**mweh**-yeh
	el	**di**·que	**dee**-keh
floating dock	el	**mue**·lle flo·**tan**·te	**mweh**-yeh floh-**tahn**-teh
dry dock	el	**di**·que **se**·co	**dee**-keh seh-koh
marina slip	el	**pues**·to	**pwehss**-toh
	el	lu·**gar**	loo-**gahr**
repair shop	el	ta·**ller** de re·pa·ra·**cio**·nes	tah-**yehr** **deh** reh-pah-rah-**syoh**-nehss
dockmaster	el	en·car·**ga**·do de **mue**·lles	ehn-kahr-**gah**-doh **deh** **mweh**-yehss

© 2000 Kathy Parsons, Spanish for Cruisers

Equipment			
cradle	la	**cu**·na	**koo**-nah
stand, support	el	so·**por**·te	soh-**pohr**-teh
ladder	la	es·ca·**le**·ra	ehss-kah-**leh**-rah
scaffolding	el	an·**da**·mio	ahn-**dah**-myoh

Services			
haul	el	sa·**ca**·do	sah-**kah**-doh
launch	el	bo·**ta**·do	boh-**tah**-doh
pressure wash	el	la·**va**·do **a** pre·**sión**	lah-**vah**-doh ah preh-**syohn**
scraping	el	ras·**pa**·do	rahss-**pah**-doh
long-term storage	el	es·ta·cio·na·**mien**·to **mu**·cho **tiem**·po	ehss-tah-syoh-nah-**myehn**-toh **moo**-choh **tyehm**-poh
short-term storage	el	es·ta·cio·na·**mien**·to **po**·co **tiem**·po	ehss-tah-syoh-nah-**myehn**-toh **poh**-koh **tyehm**-poh
... covered (under roof)		... **ba**·jo **te**·cho	**bah**-hoh **teh**-choh
do-it-yourself		**há**·ga·lo us·**ted** **mis**·mo	**ah**-gah-loh ooss-**tehd** **meess**-moh
electricity	la la	e·lec·tri·ci·**dad** **luz**	eh-lehk-tree-see-**dahd** **looss**

© 2000 Kathy Parsons, Spanish for Cruisers

Tell number of masts		
It has one mast.	**Tie**ne **un más**til.	**Tyeh**-neh **oon mahss**-teel.
It has two masts.	**Tie**ne **dos más**ti-les.	**Tyeh**-neh **dohss mahss**-tee-lehss.
It doesn't have a mast.	**No tie**ne **más**til.	**Noh tyeh**-neh **mahss**-teel.
I need (to) ...	Ne**ce**si**to** ...	Neh-seh-**see**-toh ...
... haul my boat	... sa**car mi bar**co	... sah-**kahr mee bahr**-koh
... store my sailboat	... guar**dar mi** ve**le**ro	... gwahr-**dahr mee** veh-**leh**-roh
... paint the bottom	... pin**tar el fon**do	... peen-**tahr ehl fohn**-doh
... repair ...	... repa**rar** ...	... reh-pah-**rahr** ...
... pull the mast	... sa**car el más**til	... sah-**kahr ehl mahss**-teel
... live aboard	... vi**vir a bor**do	... vee-**veer ah bohr**-doh
... launch my boat	... bo**tar mi bar**co	... boh-**tahr mee bahr**-koh
...when I return	... **cuan**do re**gre**so	... **kwahn**-doh reh-**greh**-soh
I want to haul my boat ... at ... o'clock.	**Quie**ro sa**car mi bar**co .... **a las** ...	**Kyeh**-roh sah-**kahr mee bahr**-koh ... **ah lahss** ...
What is the depth of the entrance?	¿**Cuál es la** profundi**dad de la** en**tra**da?	**Kwahl ehss lah** proh-foon-dee-**dahd deh lah** ehn-**trah**-dah?
... at high tide	... **en la** ba**ja**mar	**ehn lah** bah-hah-**mahr**
... at low tide	... **en la** plea**mar**	**ehn lah** pleh-ah-**mahr**

© 2000 Kathy Parsons, Spanish for Cruisers

How much does it cost (to)...?	¿**Cuán**to **cues**ta ...?	Kwahn-toh kwehss-tah ... ?
... haul	... sa**car**	sah-**kahr**
... launch	... bo**tar** ... e**char**	boh-**tahr** eh-**chahr**
... store	... guar**dar**	gwahr-**dahr**
... scrape the bottom	... ras**par el fon**do	rahss-**pahr ehl fohn**-doh
... pressure-wash	... lim**piar con a**gua **a** pre**sión**	leem-**pyahr** kohn ah-gwah ah preh-**syohn**
... remove the mast	... sa**car el más**til	sah-**kahr ehl mahss**-teel

How much does it cost ...?	¿**Cuán**to **cues**ta ...?	Kwahn-toh kwehss-tah ... ?
... per foot	... **por pie**	... pohr pyeh
... per hour	... **por ho**ra	... pohr oh-rah
... per day	... **por dí**a	... pohr dee-ah
... per month	... **por mes**	... pohr mehss

Is it the same price ...?	¿**Es el mis**mo **pre**cio ...?	Ehss ehl meess-moh preh-syoh ...?
... if you do the work?	... **si** us**te**des **ha**cen **el** tra**ba**jo?	... **see** ooss-**teh-dehss** ah-sehn **ehl** trah-**bah**-hoh?
... if I do the work?	... **si yo ha**go **el** tra**ba**jo?	... **see** yoh ah-goh **ehl** trah-**bah**-hoh?
... if I live a board?	... **si vi**vo **a bor**do.	... **see** vee-voh ah **bohr**-doh?

© 2000 Kathy Parsons, Spanish for Cruisers

Is everything included?	¿Está incluido todo?	Ehss-**tah** een-**klwee**-doh **toh**-doh?
How many days do I get free?	¿**Cuán**tos **dí**as **me dan gra**tis?	Kwahn-tohss **dee**-ahss **meh dahn grah**-teess?
Can I use my own paint?	¿**Pue**do u**sar mi pro**pia pin**tu**ra?	Pweh-doh oo-**sahr** mee proh-pyah peen-**too**-rah?
Do I need to buy materials here?	¿Ne**ce**si**to** com**prar los** ma**te**ria**les** a**quí**?	Neh-seh-**see**-toh kohm-**prahr** lohss mah-teh-**ryah**-lehss ah-**kee**?
I want to do all the work.	**Quie**ro ha**cer yo to**do **el** tra**ba**jo.	Kyeh-roh ah-**sehr** yoh **toh**-doh **ehl** trah-**bah**-hoh.
Can I charge this to my account?	¿**Pue**do car**gar es**to **a mi cuen**ta?	Pweh-doh kahr-**gahr** ehss-toh **ah** mee **kwehn**-tah?
Do you have security?	¿**Tie**ne se**gu**ri**dad**?	Tyeh-neh seh-goo-ree-**dahd**?
Have you had security problems?	¿**Ha** te**ni**do pro**ble**mas **de** se**gu**ri**dad**?	Ah teh-**nee**-doh proh-**bleh**-mahss **deh** seh-goo-ree-**dahd**?
Have you had any robberies here?	¿**Ha** te**ni**do **ro**bos a**quí**?	Ah teh-**nee**-doh roh-bohss ah-**kee**?
Are there bathrooms?	¿**Hay ba**ños?	Eye bah-nyohss?
Are there showers?	¿**Hay du**chas?	Eye doo-chahss?
I don't want anyone to go (climb) aboard.	**Quie**ro **que na**die **su**ba **a bor**do.	Kyeh-roh **key** nah-dyeh **soo**-bah ah **bohr**-doh.
Is everything arranged?	¿**Es**tá a**rre**gla**do to**do?	Ehss-**tah** ah-rreh-**glah**-doh **toh**-doh?

© 2000 Kathy Parsons, Spanish for Cruisers

Paint, Varnish, Coatings

paint	la	pin·tu·ra	peen-**too**-rah
bottom paint	el	**fon**·do	**fohn**-doh
	la	pin·tu·ra **de fon**·do	peen-**too**-rah **deh fohn**-doh
varnish	el	bar·**niz**	bahr-**neess**
polyurethane	el	po·liu·re·**ta**·no	poh-lee-oo-reh-**tah**-noh
enamel	el	es·**mal**·te	ehss-**mahl**-teh
... water-based		... **a ba**·se **de a**·gua	... **ah bah**-seh **deh ah**-gwah
... 2-part		... **de dos** com·po·**nen**·tes	... **deh dohss** kohm-poh-**nehn**-tehss
sealer	el	se·lla·**dor**	seh-yah-**dohr**
primer	el	pri·**ma**·rio	pree-**mah**-ryoh
coating	el	re·cu·bri·**mien**·to	reh-koo-bree-**myehn**-toh
matte finish	el	a·ca·**ba**·do **ma**·te	ah-kah-**bah**-doh **mah**-teh
glossy finish	el	a·ca·**ba**·do **bri**·llo	ah-kah-**bah**-doh **bree**-yoh
catalyst	el	ca·ta·li·za·**dor**	kah-tah-lee-sah-**dohr**
fiberglass	la	**fi**·bra **de vi**·drio	**fee**-brah **deh vee**-dryoh
resin	la	re·**si**·na	reh-**see**-nah
hardener	el	en·du·re·ce·**dor**	ehn-doo-reh-seh-**dohr**
filler	el	re·lle·na·**dor**	reh-yeh-nah-**dohr**
putty	la	ma·**si**·lla	mah-**see**-yah
	el	mas·**ti**·que	mahss-**tee**-keh
silicone sealant	el	se·lla·**dor a ba**·se **de** si·li·**cón**	seh-yah-**dohr ah bah**-seh **deh** see-lee-**kohn**

© 2000 Kathy Parsons, Spanish for Cruisers

caulk	el	sellador calafateador	seh-yah-**dohr** kah-lah-fah-teh-ah-**dohr**
solvent	el	sol**ven**te	sohl-**vehn**-teh
acetone	la	acetona	ah-seh-**toh**-nah
thinner	el	**tí**ner	**tee**-nehr
muriatic acid	el	**á**cido mu**riá**tico	ah-see-doh moo-**ryah**-tee-koh
turpentine	la	tremen**ti**na	treh-mehn-**tee**-nah
denatured alcohol	el	alco**hol** desnatura**li**za**do**	ahl-koh-**ohl** dehss-nah-too-rah-lee-**sah**-doh
mineral spirits	las	e**sen**cias mine**ra**les	eh-sehn-syahss mee-nah-**rah**-lehss
paint remover	el	remove**dor** de pin**tu**ra	reh-moh-veh-**dohr** deh peen-**too**-rah

Painting Suppplies

brush	la	**bro**cha	**broh**-chah
sponge brush	la	**bro**cha **de** es**pon**ja	**broh**-chah **deh** ehss-**pohn**-hah
roller	el	ro**di**llo	roh-**dee**-yoh
roller cover	la	cu**bier**ta	koo-**byehr**-tah
	el	**fo**rro	**foh**-rroh
sprayer	el	rocia**dor**	roh-syah-**dohr**
	el	**spray**	ehss-**preh**
air gun	la	pis**to**la **de ai**re	peess-**toh**-lah **deh eye**-reh
wire brush	el	ce**pi**llo **de** a**ce**ro	seh-**pee**-yoh deh ah-**seh**-roh
bucket	la	cu**be**ta	koo-**beh**-tah
strainer	la	cola**de**ra	koh-lah-**deh**-rah
sandpaper	el	pa**pel de li**ja	pah-**pehl deh lee**-hah

© 2000 Kathy Parsons, Spanish for Cruisers

remove the gelcoat	quitar el gelcoat	kee-**tahr** el **gel**-coat
remove the old paint	quitar la pintura vieja	kee-**tahr** lah peen-**too**-rah **vyeh**-hah
repair	reparar arreglar	reh-pah-**rahr** ah-rreh-**glahr**
repair the blisters	reparar las burbujas	reh-pah-**rahr** lahss boor-**boo**-hahss
sand	lijar	lee-**hahr**
scrape	raspar	rahss-**pahr**
seal	sellar	seh-**yahr**
spray-paint	rociar la pintura	roh-**syahr** lah peen-**too**-rah
thin	adelgazar	ah-dehl-gah-**sahr**
wait until tomorrow	esperar hasta mañana	ehss-peh-**rahr** **ahss**-tah mah-**nyah**-nah
wet sand	lijar con agua	lee-**hahr** kohn ah-**gwah**
Can I use my own paint?	¿**Pue**do u**sar mi pro**pia pin**tu**ra?	**Pweh**-doh oo-**sahr** mee proh-pyah peen-**too**-rah?
Do I need to buy materials here?	¿Ne·ce·si·to com**prar los** ma·te**ria**les a**quí**?	Neh-seh-**see**-toh kohm-**prahr lohss** mah-teh-**ryah**-lehss ah-**kee**?
I want to do all the work.	**Quie**ro ha**cer yo to**do **el** tra**ba**jo.	**Kyeh**-roh ah-**sehr yoh toh**-doh **ehl** trah-**bah**-hoh.
What brand of paint do you use?	¿**Qué mar**ca **de** pin**tu**ra **u**san us**te**des?	**Keh mahr**-kah **deh** peen-**too**-rah **oo**-sahn ooss-**teh**-dehss?
Can I charge this to my account?	¿**Pue**do car**gar es**to **a mi cuen**ta?	**Pweh**-doh kahr-**gahr ehss**-toh **ah mee kwehn**-tah?

© 2000 Kathy Parsons, Spanish for Cruisers

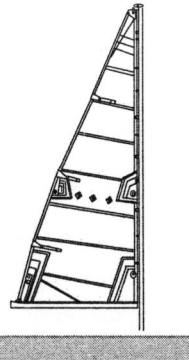 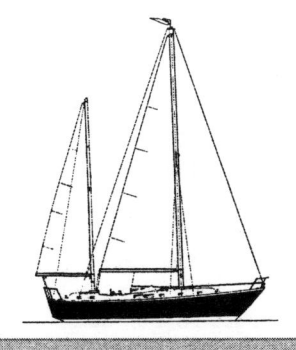

Sails			
sail	la	**ve**·la	**veh**-lah
mainsail	la	**ve**·la ma·**yor**	**veh**-lah mah-**yohr**
jib	el	**fo**·que	**foh**-keh
genoa	la	**gé**·no·va	**heh**-noh-vah
roller furler	el	en·ro·lla·**dor**	ehn-roh-yah-**dohr**
working jib	el	**fo**·que **de** tra·**ba**·jo	**foh**-keh **deh** trah-**bah**-hoh
staysail	la	**ve**·la **de** es·**tay**	**veh**-lah **deh** ehss-**teye**
mizzen	la	me·**sa**·na	meh-**sah**-nah
stormsail	el	**fo**·que **de** ca·pa	**foh**-keh **deh** kah-pah
spinnaker	el	**spin**·na·ker	ehss-**pee**-nah-kehr
	el	ba·**lón**	bah-**lohn**

© 2000 Kathy Parsons, Spanish for Cruisers

Parts of a Sail			
head	el	**pu**·ño **de dri**·za	**poo**-nyoh **deh dree**-sah
tack	el	**pu**·ño **de** a·**mu**·ra	**poo**-nyoh **deh** ah-**moo**-rah
clew	el	**pu**·ño **de** es·**co**·ta	**poo**-nyoh **deh** ehss-**koh**-tah
foot	el	**pie**	**pyeh**
luff	el	**grá**·til	**grah**-teel
leech	la	ba·**lu**·ma	bah-**loo**-mah
batten pocket	la	**bol**·sa **del** lis·**tón**	**bohl**-sah **dehl** leess-**tohn**
	la	**bol**·sa **del** sa·ble	**bohl**-sah **dehl** sah-bleh
reefs	los	**ri**·zos	**ree**-sohss
cringle	el	o·**je**·te **de** pre·**sión** *(not Mexico!)*	oh-**heh**-teh **deh** preh-**syohn**
	el	o·**ji**·llo **de** pre·**sión** *(Mexico)*	oh-**hee**-oh **deh** preh-syohn
sacrificial	la	**ban**·da **de** pro·tec·**ción UV**	**bahn**-dah **deh** proh-tehk-**syohn oo veh**
chafe protection	el	re·**fuer**·zo **con**·tra ro·za·**mien**·to	reh-**fwehr**-soh **kohn**-trah roh-sah-**myehn**-toh
cloth	la	**te**·la	**teh**-lah

© 2000 Kathy Parsons, Spanish for Cruisers

Canvas and Upholstery items

awning	el	**tol**·do	**tohl**-doh
bimini	el	**tol**·do **con tu**·bos	**tohl**-doh **kohn too**-bohss
bolster	el	tra·ve·**sa**·ño	trah-veh-**sah**-nyoh
cushion	el	co·**jín**	koh-**heen**
cushions	los	co·**jí**·nes	koh-**hee**-nehss
dodger	la	ca·**po**·ta	kah-**poh**-tah
	el	**tol**·do	**tohl**-doh
dodger (round)	la	ca·po·**ti**·na	kah-poh-**tee**-nah
mattress	el	col·**chón**	kohl-**chohn**
pillow	la	al·mo·**ha**·da	ahl-moh-**ah**-dah
pillowcase, case, cover	la	**fun**·da	**foon**-dah
plastic for windows	el	trans·pa·**ren**·te	trahnss-pah-**rehn**-teh
	el	**plás**·ti·co	**plahss**-tee-koh
sail bag	la	**bol**·sa **pa**·ra **ve**·la	**bohl**-sah **pah**-rah **veh**-lah
sail cover	la	**fun**·da **pa**·ra **ve**·la	**foon**-dah **pah**-rah **veh**-lah
window	la	ven·**ta**·na	vehn-**tah**-nah

Types of Cloth, Materials

fabric, cloth	la	**te**·la (<u>not</u> **fá**·bri·ca, **fá**·bri·ca means **factory**)	**teh**-lah
piece of cloth	el	**tro**·zo	**troh**-soh

© 2000 Kathy Parsons, Spanish for Cruisers

| canvas | la | **lo**·na | **loh**-nah |
| upholstery | la | ta·pi·ce·**rí**·a | ta-pee-seh-**ree**-ah |

See pages 63-64 for types of fabric and other materials

Sewing terms

sewing, seam	la	cos·**tu**·ra	kohss-**too**-rah
stitch	la	pun·**ta**·da	poon-**tah**-dah
lining	el	**fo**·rro	**foh**-rroh
flap	la	ce·**ne**·fa	seh-**neh**-fah
bound fabric edge, cording	el	**vi**·vo	**vee**-voh
zig-zag	el	**zig**-zag	**seeg**-sahg
edge of fabric	la	o·**ri**·lla	oh-**ree**-yah
hem	el	do·bla·**di**·llo	doh-blah-**dee**-yoh
	la	bas·**ti**·lla	bahss-**tee**-yah
layers of cloth or thicknesses	las	**ca**·pas	**kah**-pahss
patch	el	**par**·che	**pahr**-cheh
reverse side	el	re·**vés**	reh-**vehss**
right side	el	de·**re**·cho	deh-**reh**-choh
corner	la	es·**qui**·na	ehss-**kee**-nah

© 2000 Kathy Parsons, Spanish for Cruisers

padeye	el	**puen**·te	**pwehn**-teh
rope	el	**ca**·bo *(not ropa!*	**kah**-boh
	la	**so**·ga *ropa means clothes)*	**soh**-gah
slide, track	la	co·rre·**de**·ra	koh-rreh-**deh**-rah
tape	la	**cin**·ta	**seen**-tah
terminal	el	ter·mi·**nal**	tehr-mee-**nahl**
thread	el	**hi**·lo	**ee**-loh
tubing	el	**tu**·bo	**too**-boh
twist fastener	el	**bro**·che T	**broh**-cheh **teh**
velcro	el	**vel**·cro	**vehl**-kroh
zipper	la	cre·ma·**lle**·ra	kreh-mah-**yeh**-rah
	el	**zi**·per	**see**-pehr

Tools and Equipment

sewing machine	la	**má**·qui·na **de** co·**ser**	**mah**-kee-nah **deh** koh-**sehr**
scissors	las	ti·**je**·ras	tee-**heh**-rahss
needle	la	a·**gu**·ja	ah-**goo**-hah
ruler	la	**re**·gla	**reh**-glah
tape measure	la	**cin**·ta **mé**·tri·ca	**seen**-tah meh-**tree**-kah
	el	**me**·tro	**meh**-troh

© 2000 Kathy Parsons, Spanish for Cruisers

People

sailmaker	el	fabri**can**te **de ve**las	**fah-bree-kahn**-teh **deh veh**-lahss
	el	ve**le**ro *(same as sailboat)*	veh-**leh**-roh
upholsterer	el	tapi**ce**ro	tah-pee-**seh**-roh
tailor	el	**sas**tre	**sahss**-treh
seamstress	la	cos·tu**re**ra	kohss-too-**reh**-rah

Shops

fabric shop	la	**tien**da **de te**las	**tyehn**-dah **deh teh**-lahss
notions shop *(zippers, binding, etc.)*	la	**tien**da **de a**dornos	**tyehn**-dah **deh** ah-**dohr**-nohss
upholstery shop	la	tapice**ría**	tah-pee-seh-**ree**-ah
tailor's shop	la	sastre**ría**	sahss-treh-**ree**-ah
sail shop	el	ta**ller de ve**las	tah-**yehr deh veh**-lahss

I need fabric for ...	Ne·ce·si·to **te**la **pa**ra ...	Neh-seh-**see**-toh **teh-lah pah**-rah ...
What's it made of?	**¿De qué es?**	**Deh keh ehss?**
What is the width?	**¿Cuál es el an**·cho?	**Kwahl ehss ehl ahn**-choh?
How many meters are there?	**¿Cuán**·tos **me**·tros **hay?**	**Kwahn-tohss meh**-trohss **eye?**
Is it waterproof?	**¿Es** im·per·me·a·ble?	**Ehss** eem-pehr-meh-**ah**-bleh?
Are there other colors?	**¿Hay o**·tros co·lo·res?	**Eye** oh-trohss koh-**loh**-rehss?
Do you have the fabric?	**¿Tie**·ne **la te**la?	**Tyeh**-neh **lah teh**-lah?

© 2000 Kathy Parsons, Spanish for Cruisers

I need something ...	Necesito algo ...	Neh-seh-**see**-toh **ahl**-goh ...
... heavier	... **más** pesado	... **mahss** peh-**sah**-doh
... wider	... **más** ancho	... **mahss ahn**-choh
... with UV protection	... **con** protec**ción** UV	... **kohn** proh-tehk-**syohn** **oo** **veh**

I want ...	Quiero ...	Kyeh-roh ...
... a new awning ..	... **un nue**vo **tol**do ...	... **oon nweh**-voh **tohl**-doh ...
... exactly like this	... igual a este	... ee-**gwahl** ah **ehss**-teh ...
... like this but ...	... como este pero ...	... **koh**-moh **ehss**-teh **peh**-roh ...
... x meters long	... **de** x **me**tros **de lar**go	... **deh** ... **meh**-trohss **deh lahr**-goh
... x meters wide	... **de** x **me**tros **de an**cho	... **deh** ... **meh**-trohss **deh ahn**-choh
... x meters tall	... **de** x **me**tros **de al**to	... **deh** ... **meh**-trohss **deh ahl**-toh
... with grommets in the corners	... **con** ojetes (oji**llos** - Mex) **en las** esquinas	... **kohn** oh-**heh**-tehss (oh-**hee**-yohss) **ehn las** ehss-**kee**-nahss

The sail is ...	La vela está ...	Lah **veh**-lah ehss-**tah** ...
... torn	... **ro**ta	... **roh**-tah
... needs restitching (un-stitched)	... descosida	... dehss-koh-**see**-dah
... worn-out	... gastada	... gahss-**tah**-dah

© 2000 Kathy Parsons, Spanish for Cruisers

To talk about what kind of sails or upholstery work you need, add an ACTION PHRASE to the SENTENCE and QUESTIONS STARTERS below.

Sentence Starters

How much does it cost (to) ... ?	¿Cuánto cuesta ...?	Kwahn-toh kwehss-tah ... ?
Can you ...?	¿Puede ...?	Pweh-deh ...?
When can you ...?	¿Cuándo puede ...?	Kwahn-doh pweh-deh ...?
How long (will it take) to...?	¿Cuánto tiempo para ...?	Kwahn-toh tyehm-poh pah-rah ...?
I want (to) ...	Quiero ...	Kyeh-roh ...
I need (to) ...	Necesito ...	Neh-seh-see-toh ...
You need (to) ...	Necesita ...	Neh-seh-see-tah ...

Action Phrases

cover ...	cubrir ...	koo-breer
cut ...	cortar ...	kohr-tahr
fasten ...	sujetar ...	soo-heh-tahr
make ...	hacer ...	ah-sehr
make this bigger	hacer esto más grande	ah-sehr ehss-toh mahss grahn-deh
make this longer	hacer esto más largo	ah-sehr ehss-toh mahss lahr-goh
make this shorter	hacer esto más corto	ah-sehr ehss-toh mahss kohr-toh
make this smaller	hacer esto más pequeño	ah-sehr ehss-toh mahss peh-keh-nyoh

© 2000 Kathy Parsons, Spanish for Cruisers

make this stronger	ha·**cer es**·to **más fuer**·te	ah-**sehr ehss**-toh **mahss fwehr**-teh
measure	me·**dir** ...	meh-**deer**
order the fabric	or·de·**nar la te**·la	ohr-deh-**nahr lah teh**-lah
patch, mend	re·men·**dar** ...	reh-mehn-**dahr**
put a patch on ...	po·**ner un par**·che **en** ...	poh-**nehr oon pahr**-cheh **ehn**
put on ...	po·**ner** ...	poh-**nehr**
reinforce	re·for·**zar** ...	reh-fohr-**sahr**
repair ...	re·pa·**rar** ...	reh-pah-**rahr**
replace ...	cam·**biar** ...	kahm-**byahr**
restitch ...	re·co·**ser** ...	reh-koh-**sehr**
sew, stitch	co·**ser** ...	koh-**sehr**
take the measurements of ...	to·**mar las** me·**di**·das **a** ...	toh-**mahr lahss** meh-**dee**-dahss **ah**
tie	a·ma·**rrar**	ah-mah-**rrahr**
tighten	ten·**sar** ...	tehn-**sahr**
use ...	u·**sar** ...	oo-**sahr**

Examples

Can you + restitch the genoa?	¿**Pue**·de + re·co·**ser la gé**·no·va?
How much does it cost to + replace the zippers?	¿**Cuán**·to **cues**·ta + cam·**biar las** cre·ma·**lle**·ras?
You need to + make this bigger.	Ne·ce·**si**·ta + ha·**cer es**·to **más gran**·de.
I want to + use this foam rubber.	**Quie**·ro + u·**sar es**·ta **go**·ma es·**pu**·ma.

© 2000 Kathy Parsons, Spanish for Cruisers

drill, electric	el	ta·la·dro e·léc·tri·co	tah-**lah**-droh eh-**lehk**-tree-koh
drill, hand	el	ta·la·dro **de ma**·no	tah-**lah**-droh **deh mah**-noh
drill bit	la	**me**·cha *(Venezuela)*	**meh**-chah
	la	**bro**·ca *(Mexico)*	**broh**-kah
drill press	el	ta·la·dro **de pie**	tah-**lah**-droh **deh pyeh**
feeler gauge	el	ca·li·bra·**dor de cin**·ta	kah-lee-brah-**dohr deh seen**-tah
file	la	**li**·ma	**lee**-mah
flare tool	el	a·ve·lla·na·**dor**	ah-veh-yah-nah-**dohr**
	el	a·bo·car·da·**dor**	ah-boh-kahr-dah-**dohr**
flashlight	la	lin·**ter**·na	leen-**tehr**-nah
	el	**fo**·co	**foh**-koh
	la	**lám**·pa·ra	**lahm**-pah-rah
funnel	el	em·**bu**·do	ehm-**boo**-doh
gauge	el	in·di·ca·**dor**	een-dee-kah-**dohr**
	el	me·di·**dor**	meh-dee-**dohr**
gauge, pressure	el	ma·**nó**·me·tro	mah-**noh**-meh-troh
gloves	los	**guan**·tes	**gwahn**-tehss
grease gun	el	en·gra·sa·**dor**	ehn-grah-sah-**dohr**
grinder	el	es·me·**ril**	ehss-meh-**reel**
grinder, bench	el	es·me·**ril de ban**·co	ehss-meh-**reel deh bahn**-koh
hacksaw	la	se·**gue**·ta	seh-**gheh**-tah
hacksaw blade	la	**ho**·ja **pa**·ra se·**gue**·ta	oh-hah **pah**-rah seh-**gheh**-tah

© 2000 Kathy Parsons, Spanish for Cruisers

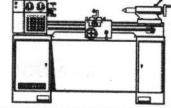   

"Why do you call a hoist a señorita?"
I asked the Venezuelan engineer. "
—"Because it can lift anything" he
replied.

hammer	el	martillo	mahr-**tee**-yoh
heat gun	la	pistola **tér**mica	peess-**toh**-lah **tehr**-mee-kah
hoist	el	monta**car**gas	mohn-tah-**kahr**-gahss
	la	señorita *(Venezuela)*	seh-nyoh-**ree**-tah
jack	el	**ga**to	**gah**-toh
knife	el	cu**chi**llo	koo-**chee**-yoh
knife (penknife)	la	na**va**ja	nah-**vah**-hah
lathe	el	**tor**no	**tohr**-noh
level	el	ni**vel**	nee-**vehl**
mallet, rubber	el	martillo **de go**ma	mahr-**tee**-yoh **deh goh**-mah
mask	la	**más**cara	**mahss**-kah-rah
metal shears	la	ci**za**lla	see-**sah**-yah
milling machine	la	fresa**do**ra	freh-sah-**doh**-rah
multimeter	el	mul**tí**metro	mool-**tee**-meh-troh
paint brush	la	**bro**cha	**broh**-chah
paint roller	el	ro**di**llo **de** pin**tar**	roh-dee-yoh **deh** peen-**tahr**
paint roller cover	la	cu**bier**ta **del** ro**di**llo	koo-**byehr**-tah **dehl** roh-**dee**-yoh
	el	**fo**rro **del** ro**di**llo	**foh**-rroh **dehl** roh-**dee**-yoh

© 2000 Kathy Parsons, Spanish for Cruisers

paint roller tray	la	ban·**de**·ja	bahn-**deh**-hah
	la	cha·**ro**·la	chah-**roh**-lah
pipe cutter	el	corta·**tu**·bos	kohr-tah-**too**-bohss
pliers	los	a·li·**ca**·tes *(Carib)*	al-lee-**kah**-tehss
	las	**pin**·zas *(Mexico)*	**peen**-sahss
pliers, crimping	las	te·**na**·zas co·nec·**to**·ras	teh-**nah**-sahss koh-nehk-**toh**-rahss
pliers, needle-nose	las	**pin**·zas **de** **pun**·tas	**peen**-sahss **deh** **poon**-tahss
putty knife	la	es·**pá**·tu·la	ehss-**pah**-too-lah
razor blade	la	na·**va**·ja de ra·su·**rar**	nah-**vah**-hah **deh** rah-soo-**rahr**
riveter	la	re·ma·cha·**do**·ra	reh-mah-chah-**doh**-rah
ruler	la	**re**·gla	**reh**-glah
safety glasses	los	**len**·tes de se·gu·ri·**dad**	**lehn**-tehss **deh** seh-goo-ree-**dahd**
sander	la	li·ja·**do**·ra	lee-hah-**doh**-rah
sanding disk	el	**dis**·co **pa**·ra li·**jar**	**deess**-koh **pah**-rah lee-**hahr**
sandpaper	el	pa·**pel** **de** **li**·ja	pah-**pehl** **deh** **lee**-hah
saw	la	**sie**·rra	**syeh**-rrah
scissors	las	ti·**je**·ras	tee-**heh**-rahss
scraper	la	es·**pá**·tu·la	ehss-**pah**-too-lah
	el	ras·pa·**dor**	rahss-pah-**dohr**
screwdriver	el	des·tor·ni·lla·**dor** *(Caribbean)*	dehss-tohr-nee-yah-**dohr**
	el	des·ar·ma·**dor** *(Mexico)*	dehss-ahr-mah-**dohr**

© 2000 Kathy Parsons, Spanish for Cruisers

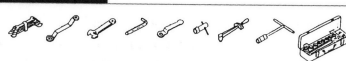

screwdriver, flat	el	des·tor·ni·lla**dor pla**·no *(Carib)*	dehss-tohr-nee-yah-**dohr plah**-noh
	el	des·ar·ma**dor pla**·no *(Mexico)*	dehss-ahr-mah-**dohr plah**-noh
screwdriver, Phillips	el	des·tor·ni·lla**dor de es·trí**·a *(Carib)*	dehss-tohr-nee-yah-**dohr deh** ehss-**tree**-ah
	el	des·ar·ma**dor de cruz** *(Mexico)*	dehss-ahr-mah-**dohr deh krooss**
socket	el	**da**·do	**dah**-doh
solder	la	sol·da**du**·ra	sohl-dah-**doo**-rah
soldering flux	el	fun·**den**·te **pa**·ra sol·**dar**	foon-**dehn**-teh **pah**-rah sohl-**dahr**
solder gun	la	sol·da**do**·ra	sohl-dah-**doh**-rah
strainer	la	co·la**de**·ra	koh-lah-**deh**-rah
tap *(for creating threads)*	el	ma**chue**·lo	mah-**chweh**-loh
	el	**ma**·cho **pa**·ra ha·**cer ros**·cas	**mah**-choh **pah**-rah ah-**sehr rohss**-kahss
tape	la	**cin**·ta	**seen**-tah
	el	**tei**·pe *(Venezuela)*	**teh**-peh
tape measure	la	**cin**·ta **pa**·ra me·**dir**	**seen**-tah **pah**-rah meh-**deer**
tin snips	las	ti·**je**·ras **pa**·ra cor·**tar lá**·mi·na	tee-**heh**-rahss **pah**-rah kohr-**tahr** lah-mee-nah
tool	la	he·rra·**mien**·ta	eh-rah-**myehn**-tah
vise	el	tor·**ni**·llo **de ban**·co	tohr-**nee**-yoh **deh bahn**-koh
vise-grips	los	a·li·**ca**·tes **de** pre·**sión** *(Caribbean)*	ah-lee-**kah**-tehss **deh** preh-**syohn**
	las	**pin**·zas **de** pre·**sión** *(Mexico)*	**peen**-sahss **deh** preh-**syohn**

© 2000 Kathy Parsons, Spanish for Cruisers

voltmeter	el	voltímetro	vohl-**tee**-meh-troh
welding torch	el	soplete soldador	soh-**pleh**-teh sohl-dah-**dohr**
wheel puller	el	extractor de ruedas	ehkss-trahk-**tohr deh rweh**-dahss
wire brush	el	cepillo de alambre	seh-**pee**-yoh **deh** ah-**lahm**-breh
wire strippers	los	alicates pelacables	ah-lee-**kah**-tehss peh-lah-**kah**-blehss
wire-cutters	el	cortacables	kohr-tah-**kah**-blehss
wrench	la	**lla**ve	**yah-veh**
wrench, Allen	la	**lla**ve **de** Allen	**yah-veh deh** ah-lehn
wrench, box end	la	**lla**ve cerrada	**yah-veh** seh-**rrah**-dah
wrench, crescent	la	**lla**ve ajustable	**yah-veh** ah-hooss-**tah**-bleh
	el	perico	peh-**ree**-koh
wrench, hex	la	**lla**ve hexagonal	**yah-veh** ehks-ah-goh-**nahl**
wrench, oil filter	la	**lla**ve para filtro de aceite	**yah-veh** pah-rah **feel**-troh **deh** ah-**say**-teh
wrench, open end	la	**lla**ve **de** boca	**yah-veh deh** boh-kah
wrench, pipe	la	**lla**ve **de** tubos	**yah-veh deh too**-bohss
	la	**lla**ve **Stil**son	**yah-veh** eh-**steel**-sohn
wrench, ratchet	la	**lla**ve **de** trinquete	**yah-veh deh** treen-**keh**-teh
	la	**rat**chet	**raht**-cheht
	el	maneral	mah-neh-**rahl**
wrench, socket	la	**lla**ve **de** dado	**yah-veh deh** dah-doh
wrench, spark plug	la	**lla**ve para bujía	**yah-veh** pah-rah boo-**hee**-ah
wrench, torque	la	**lla**ve **de** torsión	**yah-veh deh** tohr-**syohn**

© 2000 Kathy Parsons, Spanish for Cruisers

© 2000 Kathy Parsons, Spanish for Cruisers

© 2000 Kathy Parsons, Spanish for Cruisers

© 2000 Kathy Parsons, Spanish for Cruisers

© 2000 Kathy Parsons, Spanish for Cruisers

© 2000 Kathy Parsons, Spanish for Cruisers

© 2000 Kathy Parsons, Spanish for Cruisers

© 2000 Kathy Parsons, Spanish for Cruisers

© 2000 Kathy Parsons, Spanish for Cruisers

These words will come in handy to refer to the job, parts, and repairs needed.

Jobs, Parts, Repairs

this *(great to use when you don't know the word!)*		**es**to	**ehss**-toh
work, job	el	tra**ba**jo	trah-**bah**-hoh
repair	el	a**rre**glo	ah-**rreh**-gloh
part	la	**pie**za	**pyeh**-sah
replacement or spare part	el	re**pues**to	reh-**pwehss**-toh
replacement or spare part *(Mexico)*	la	refac**ción**	reh-fahk-**syohn**
labor	la	**ma**no **de o**bra	**mah**-noh **deh** oh-brah

Can you repair this?

Can you repair the motor?	¿**Pue**de re**pa**rar **el** mo**tor**?	**Pweh**-deh reh-pah-**rahr** ehl moh-**tohr**?
Have you worked with this type of motor before?	¿**Ha** tra·ba**ja**do **con es**te **ti**po **de** mo**tor an**tes?	Ah trah-bah-**hah**-doh **kohn** ehss-teh **tee**-poh **deh** moh-**tohr** ahn-tehss?
Is there another place where they can repair this?	¿**Hay o**tro lu**gar don**de **pue**de re**pa**rar **es**to?	**Eye** oh-troh loo-**gahr dohn**-deh **pweh**-deh reh-pah-**rahr ehss**-toh?
Who can repair this?	¿**Quién pue**de re**pa**rar **es**to?	**Kyehn** pweh-deh reh-pah-**rahr ehss**-toh?

© 2000 Kathy Parsons, Spanish for Cruisers

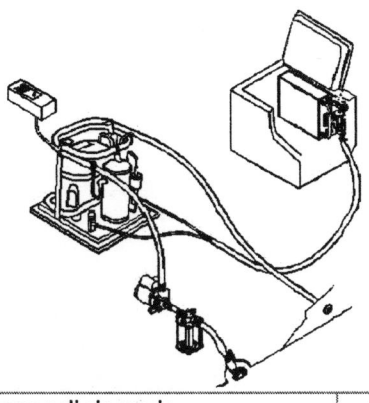

air conditioning	el	**ai**·re a·con·di·cio·**na**·do	**eye**-reh ah-kohn-dee-syoh-**nah**-doh
refrigeration	la	re·fri·ge·ra·**ción**	reh-free-heh-rah-**syohn**
refrigerator	el	re·fri·ge·ra·**dor**	reh-free-heh-rah-**dohr**
...engine-driven		...im·pul·**sa**·do **por el** mo·**tor del bar**·co	eem-pool-**sah**-doh **pohr ehl** moh-**tohr dehl bahr**-koh
...12 volt		... **de do**·ce **vol**·tios	...**deh doh**-seh **vohl**-tyohss
...120 volt		... **de cien**·to **vein**·te **vol**·tios	...**de syehn**-toh **vayn**-teh **vohl**-tyohss
accumulator	el	a·cu·mu·la·**dor**	ah-koo-moo-lah-**dohr**
capillary tube	el	**tu**·bo ca·pi·**lar**	**too**-boh kah-pee-**lahr**
charging valve	la	**vál**·vu·la **de car**·ga	**vahl**-voo-lah **deh kahr**-gah

© 2000 Kathy Parsons, Spanish for Cruisers

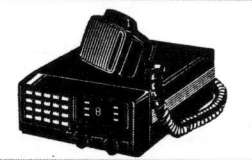
Radios

English	Art.	Spanish	Pronunciation
radio	la	**ra**·dio	**rah**-dyoh
VHF radio	la	**ra**·dio **V·H·F**	**rah**-dyoh **Veh Ah**-cheh **Eh**-feh
HF radio	la	**ra**·dio **H·F**	**rah**-dyoh **Ah**-cheh **Eh**-feh
SSB radio	la	**ra**·dio **S·S·B**	**rah**-dyoh **Eh**-seh **Eh**-seh **Beh**
transceiver	el	trans·re·cep**tor**	trahnss-reh-sehp-**tohr**
2-meter radio	la	**ra**·dio **de dos me**·tros	**rah**-dyoh **deh dohss meh**-trohss
radio beacon	la	**ra**·dio ba·**li**·za	rah-dyoh bah-**lee**-sah
cellular telephone	el	te·**lé**·fo·no ce·lu·**lar**	teh-**leh**-foh-noh seh-loo-**lahr**
short-wave	la	... **on**·da **cor**·ta	... **ohn**-dah **kohr**-tah
...portable		... por·**tá**·til	... pohr-**tah**-teel
...fixed (installation)		... **fi**·ja	... **fee**-hah

Components

English	Art.	Spanish	Pronunciation
antenna	la	an·**te**·na	ahn-**teh**-nah
insulated backstay	la	**bur**·da ais·**la**·da	**boor**-dah eyess-**lah**-dah
coaxial cable	el	**ca**·ble co·a·**xial**	**kah**-bleh koh-ahk-**syahl**
ground cable	el	**ca**·ble **de tie**·rra	**kah**-bleh **deh tyeh**-rrah

© 2000 Kathy Parsons, Spanish for Cruisers

short circuit	el	corto circuito	kohr-toh-seer-**kwee**-toh
open circuit	el	circuito abierto	seer-**kwee**-toh ah-**byehr**-toh
low voltage	el	voltaje bajo	vohl-**tah**-heh **bah**-hoh
blown fuse	el	fusible fundido	foo-**see**-bleh foon-**dee**-doh
bad ground	la	**tie**rra **ma**la	**tyeh**-rrah **mah**-lah
loose connection	la	conexión suelta	koh-nehk-**syohn swehl**-tah
installation	la	instalación	een-stah-lah-**syohn**
voltage drop	la	caída de voltaje	kah-**ee**-dah **deh** vohl-**tah**-heh
plugged in		enchufado	ehn-choo-**fah**-doh
unplugged		desenchufado	dehss-ehn-choo-**fah**-doh
on		prendido	prehn-**dee**-doh
		encendido	ehn-sehn-**dee**-doh
off		apagado	ah-pah-**gah**-doh

© 2000 Kathy Parsons, Spanish for Cruisers

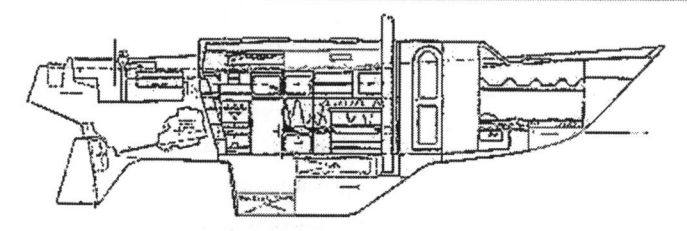
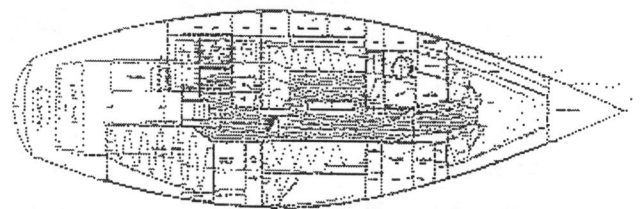

Below deck			
cabin	la	ca·**bi**·na	kah-**bee**-nah
	el	ca·ma·**ro**·te	kah-mah-**roh**-teh
bilge	la	sen·**ti**·na	sehn-**tee**-nah
chart table	la	**me**·sa **de car**·tas	**meh**-sah **deh** kahr-tahss
engine compartment	el	**cuar**·to **de má**·qui·nas	**kwahr**-toh **deh** mah-kee-nahss
engine room	la	**sa**·la **de má**·qui·nas	**sah**-lah **deh** mah-kee-nahss
galley	la	co·**ci**·na	koh-**see**-nah
bathroom	el	**ba**·ño	**bah**-nyoh
floor, sole	el	**pi**·so	**pee**-soh
toilet	el	i·no·**do**·ro	ee-noh-**doh**-roh
	el	sa·ni·**ta**·rio	sah-nee-**tah**-ryoh
bunk	la	li·**te**·ra	lee-**teh**-rah
bulkhead	el	mam·**pa**·ro	mahm-**pah**-roh
water tank	el	**tan**·que **de a**·gua	**tahn**-keh **deh** ah-gwah

© 2000 Kathy Parsons, Spanish for Cruisers

Can you ...?

Can you haul and launch ...	¿**Pue**de sa**car** y bo**tar** ..	Pweh-deh sah-**kahr** ee boh-**tahr** ...
... a sailboat ...	... **un** ve·le·ro ...	... oon veh-**leh**-roh ...
...of ... feet in length?	... **de** ... **pies** de es·lo·ra?	... deh ... pyehss ... deh ehss-loh-rah?

Describe type of boat

It is a sailboat.	**Es un** ve·le·ro.	Ehss oon veh-**leh**-roh.
It is a motor yacht.	**Es un** ya·te **de** mo·tor.	Ehss oon yah-teh **deh** moh-**tohr**.
It is a monohull.	**Es un** mo·no·**cas**·co.	Ehss oon moh-noh-**kahss**-koh.
It is a catamaran.	**Es un** ca·ta·ma·**rán**.	Ehss oon kah-tah-mah-**rahn**.

Give your length, draft and beam

The length is .... meters.	**La** es·lo·ra **es** .... **me**·tros.	Lah ehss-loh-rah ehss ..... **meh**-trohss.
The length is .... feet.	**La** es·lo·ra **es** .... **pies**.	Lah ehss-loh-rah ehss ..... **pyehss**.
The draft is .... meters.	**El** ca·la·do **es** .... **me**·tros.	Ehl kah-lah-doh ehss ..... **meh**-trohss.
The beam is .... meters.	**La man**·ga **es** .... **me**·tros.	Lah **mahn**-gah ehss ... **meh**-trohss.
The height is .... meters.	**La** al·tu·ra **es** .... **me**·tros.	Lah ahl-**too**-rah ehss .... **meh**-trohss.
The weight is ... tons.	**El pe**·so **es** .... to·ne·la·das.	Ehl **peh**-soh ehss ... toh-neh-lah-dahss.

© 2000 Kathy Parsons, Spanish for Cruisers

Sentence starters		
How much does it cost (to) ... ?	¿**Cuán**to **cues**ta ...?	**Kwahn**-toh **kwehss**-tah ... ?
Can you ...?	¿**Pue**de ...?	**Pweh**-deh ...?
When can you ...?	¿**Cuán**do **pue**de ...?	**Kwahn**-doh **pweh**-deh ...?
How long (will it take) to ...?	¿**Cuán**to **tiem**po **pa**ra ...?	**Kwahn**-toh **tyehm**-poh **pah**-rah ...?
I need (to) ...	Ne·ce·si·to ...	Neh-seh-**see**-toh ...
I don't want (to) ...	**No quie**ro ...	Noh **kyeh**-roh ...

Add these to any sentence starter above:		
clean the bottom	lim·**piar** el **fon**·do	leem-**pyahr** ehl **fohn**-doh
dry the bottom	se·**car** el **fon**·do	seh-**kahr** ehl **fohn**-doh
fill the blisters	re·lle·**nar** las bur·**bu**·jas	reh-yeh-**nahr** lahss boor-**boo**-hahss
finish today	ter·mi·**nar hoy**	tehr-mee-**nahr** oy
grind	pu·**lir**	poo-**leer**
mix the paint	mez·**clar** la pin·**tu**·ra	mess-**klahr** lah peen-**too**-rah
paint the bottom	pin·**tar** el **fon**·do	peen-**tahr** ehl **fohn**-doh
polish	pu·**lir**	poo-**leer**
prepare the surface	pre·pa·**rar** las su·per·**fi**·cies	preh-pah-**rah** lahss soo-per-**fee**-syehss
pressure-wash	lim·**piar** con **a**·gua a pre·**sión**	leem-**pyahr** kohn ah-gwah ah preh-**syohn**
put on 2 coats of paint	po·**ner dos ma**·nos de pin·**tu**·ra	poh-**nehr** dohss **mah**-nohss **deh** peen-**too**-rah

© 2000 Kathy Parsons, Spanish for Cruisers

Hardware and supplies

base *(of awning tubing, etc.)*	el	**ba**·se	**bah**-seh
bias	el	**ses**·go	**sehss**-goh
binding, edging	el	ri·**be**·te	ree-**beh**-teh
buckle	la	he·**bi**·lla	eh-**bee**-yah
button	el	bo·**tón**	boh-**tohn**
cord	la	**cuer**·da	**kwehr**-dah
	el	cor·**dón**	kohr-**dohn**
cording	el	**vi**·vo	**vee**-voh
dot fastener	el	**bro**·che **de** pre·**sión** sen·**ci**·llo	**broh**-cheh **deh** preh-**syohn** sehn-**see**-yoh
fastener	el	**bro**·che	**broh**-cheh
	el	cor·**che**·te	kohr-**cheh**-teh
grommet	el	o·**je**·te *(do not use in Mexico!)*	oh-**heh**-teh
	el	o·**ji**·llo *(Mexico)*	oh-**hee**-yoh
hook	el	**gan**·cho	**gahn**-choh
latch	la	ce·rra·**du**·ra	seh-rrah-**doo**-rah

© 2000 Kathy Parsons, Spanish for Cruisers

ammeter	el	amperímetro	ahm-peh-**ree**-meh-troh
blow torch	el	soplete	soh-**pleh**-teh
calipers	los	calibres	kah-**lee**-brehss
caulk gun	la	pistola para sellar	peess-**toh**-lah **pah**-rah seh-**yahr**
center punch	el	centro punzón	**sehn**-troh poon-**sohn**
circuit tester	el	probador de circuitos	proh-bah-**dohr deh** seer-**kwee**-tohss
clamp	el	sargento	sahr-**hehn**-toh
clamp, hook	la	grapa	**grah**-pah
chisel	el	cincel	seen-**sehl**
cold chisel	el	cortafrío	kohr-tah-**free**-oh
compressor	el	compresor	kohm-preh-**sohr**
crow bar	la	pata de cabra	**pah**-tah **deh** kah-brah
compression tester	el	medidor de compresión	meh-dee-**dohr deh** kohm-preh-**syohn**
die *(for creating threads)*	el	dado	**dah**-doh
die tool *(for creating threads)*	la	tarraja	tah-**rrah**-hah
drill	el	taladro	tah-**lah**-droh
drill, air	el	taladro de aire	tah-**lah**-droh **deh eye**-ray

© 2000 Kathy Parsons, Spanish for Cruisers

© 2000 Kathy Parsons, Spanish for Cruisers

© 2000 Kathy Parsons, Spanish for Cruisers

© 2000 Kathy Parsons, Spanish for Cruisers

© 2000 Kathy Parsons, Spanish for Cruisers

© 2000 Kathy Parsons, Spanish for Cruisers

© 2000 Kathy Parsons, Spanish for Cruisers

© 2000 Kathy Parsons, Spanish for Cruisers